Lacanian Psychotherapy with Children

THE LACANIAN CLINICAL FIELD

Lacanian Psychotherapy with Children: The Broken Piano

Catherine Mathelin

TRANSLATED BY
Susan Fairfield

NOTES BY
Judith Feher-Gurewich

OTHER
Other Press
New York

This work, published as part of the program of aid for publication, received support from the Ministry of Foreign Affairs of the Cultural Service of the French Embassy in the United States. *Cet ouvrage publié dans le cadre du programme d'aide à la publication bénéficie du soutien du Ministère des Affaires Etrangères du Service Culturel de l'Ambassade de France représenté aux Etats-Unis.*

Production Editor: Robert D. Hack

This book was set in 11 pt. Berkeley by Alpha Graphics of Pittsfield, New Hampshire.

Library of Congress Cataloging-in-Publication Data

Mathelin, Catherine.
    [Raisins verts et dents agacées. English]
    Lacanian psychotherapy with children : the broken piano /
Catherine Mathelin ; translated by Susan Fairfield ; noted by Judith
Feher-Gurewich.
        p.   cm. — (The Lacanian clinical field)
    Includes bibliographical references and index.
    ISBN 1-892746-01-8 (softcover : alk. paper)
    1. Child analysis—Case studies.   2. Lacan, Jacques, 1901–
1. Title. II. Series.
RJ504.2.M3913   1999
618.92'8917—DC21   98-36956

To Émilie and Mathieu

Acknowledgements

Above all I want to thank the children and their families who made this work possible. I am also grateful to:

Maud Mannoni, without whom this book could never have existed; Françoise Dolto, Rosine and Robert Lefort, and Solange Faladé, whose teaching has had a special influence on my work over the past twenty years; Colette Misrahi, who kindly read the proofs and whose advice, analytic rigor, and friendship were, as always, of inestimable help; Alain Vanier, with whom I have worked for such a long time that he will once again recognize here the imprint of his seminar and of our colleagueship; Dominique and Patrick Guyomard and my fellow analysts from the Centre de formation et de recherches psychanalytiques (Center for Psychoananalytic Training and Research), all of whom I cannot name here but who shared with me the adventure of creating the Center and whose participation in groups, seminars, and workshops was of great help in the preparation of this book; and last but not least Myriam El Hefnaoui, who, thanks to her patience and her kind collaboration, managed to decipher my hieroglyphics.

Catherine Mathelin, 1994

Contents

PART II
FROM THE FIRST SESSION
TO THE ANALYTIC TREATMENT

PART III
THE CLEVER BABY

The Lacanian Clinical Field:
Series Overview

Lacanian psychoanalysis exists, and the new series, The Lacanian Clinical Field, is here to prove it. The clinical expertise of French practitioners deeply influenced by the thought of Jacques Lacan has finally found a publishing home in the United States. Books that have been acclaimed in France, Italy, Spain, Greece, South America, and Japan for their clarity, didactic power, and clinical relevance will now be at the disposal of the American psychotherapeutic and academic communities. These books cover a range of topics, including theoretical introductions; clinical approaches to neurosis, perversion, and psychosis; child psychoanalysis; conceptualizations of femininity; psychoanalytic readings of American literature; and more. Thus far nine books are in preparation.

Though all these works are clinically relevant, they will also be of great interest to those American scholars who have taught and used Lacan's theories for over a decade. What better opportunity for the academic world of literary criticism, philosophy, human sciences, women's studies, film studies, and multicultural studies finally to have access to the clinical insights of a theorist known primarily for his revolutionary vision of the formation of the human subject. Thus The Lacanian Clinical Field goes beyond introducing the American clinician to a different psychoanalytic outlook. It brings together two communities that have grown progressively estranged from each other. For indeed, the time when the Frankfurt School, Lionel Trilling, Erich Fromm, Herbert Marcuse, Philip Rieff, and others were fostering exchanges between the academic and the psychoanalytic communities is gone, and in the process psychoanalysis has lost some of its vibrancy.

The very limited success of ego psychology in bringing psychoanalysis into the domain of science has left psychoanalysis in need of a metapsychology that is able not only to withstand the pernicious challenges of psychopharmacology and psychiatry but also to accommodate the findings of cognitive and developmental psychology. Infant research has put many of Freud's insights into question, and the attempts to replace a one-body psychology with a more interpersonal or intersubjective approach have led to dissension within the psychoanalytic community. Many theorists are of the opinion that the road toward scientific legitimacy requires a certain allegiance with Freud's detractors, who are convinced that the unconscious and its sexual underpinnings are merely an aberration. Psychoanalysis continues to be practiced, however, and according to both patients and analysts the uncovering of unconscious motivations continues to provide a sense of relief. But while there has been a burgeoning of different psychoanalytic schools of thought since the desacralization of Freud, no theoretical agreement has been reached as to why such relief occurs.

Nowadays it can sometimes seem that Freud is read much more scrupulously by literary critics and social scientists than by psychoanalysts. This is not entirely a coincidence. While the psychoanalytic community is searching for a new metapsychology, the human sciences have acquired a level of theoretical sophistication and complexity that has enabled them to read Freud under a new lens. Structural linguistics and structural anthropology have transformed conventional appraisals of human subjectivity and have given Freud's unconscious a new status. Lacan's teachings, along with the works of Foucault and Derrida, have been largely responsible for the explosion of new ideas that have enhanced the interdisciplinary movement pervasive in academia today.

The downside of this remarkable intellectual revolution, as far as psychoanalysis is concerned, is the fact that Lacan's contribution has been derailed from its original trajectory. No longer perceived as a theory meant to enlighten the practice of psychoanalysis, his brilliant formulations have been both adapted and criticized so as to conform to the needs of purely intellectual endeavors far removed from clinical reality. This state of affairs is certainly in part responsible for Lacan's dismissal by the psychoanalytic community. Moreover, Lacan's "impossible" style has been seen as yet another proof of the culture of obscurantism that French intellectuals seem so fond of.

In this context the works included in The Lacanian Clinical Field should serve as an eye-opener at both ends of the spectrum. The authors in the series are primarily clinicians eager to offer to professionals in psychoanalysis, psychiatry, psychology, and other mental-health disciplines a clear and succinct didactic view of Lacan's work. Their goal is not so much to emphasize the radically new insights of the Lacanian theory of subjectivity and its place in the history of human sciences as it is to show how this difficult and complex body of ideas can enhance clinical work. Therefore, while the American clinician will be made aware that Lacanian psychoanalysis is not primarily a staple of literary criticism or philosophy but a praxis meant to cure patients of their psychic distress, the academic community will be exposed for the first time to a reading of Lacan that is in sharp contrast with the literature that has thus far informed them about his theory. In that sense Lacan's teachings return to the clinical reality to which they primarily belong.

Moreover, the clinical approach of the books in this series will shed a new light on the critical amendments that literary scholars and feminist theoreticians have brought to Lacan's conceptualization of subjectivity. While Lacan has been applauded for having offered an alternative to Freud's biological determinism, he has also been accused of nevertheless remaining phallocentric in his formulation of sexual difference. Yet this criticism, one that may be valid outside of the clinical reality—psychoanalysis is both an ingredient and an effect of culture—may not have the same relevance in the clinical context. For psychoanalysis as a praxis has a radically different function from the one it currently serves in academic discourse. In the latter, psychoanalysis is perceived both as an ideology fostering patriarchal beliefs and as a theoretical tool for constructing a vision of the subject no longer dependent on a phallocratic system. In the former, however, the issue of phallocracy loses its political impact. Psychoanalytic practice can only retroactively unravel the ways in which the patient's psychic life has been constituted, and in that sense it can only reveal the function the phallus plays in the psychic elaboration of sexual difference.

The Lacanian Clinical Field, therefore, aims to undo certain prejudices that have affected Lacan's reputation up to now in both the academic and the psychoanalytic communities. While these prejudices stem from rather different causes—Lacan is perceived as too patriarchal and reactionary in the one and too far removed from clinical reality in the other—they both seem to overlook the fact that the fifty years that cover the period of Lacan's teachings were mainly devoted to working and reworking the meaning and function of psychoanalysis, not necessarily as a science or even as a human science, but as a practice that can nonetheless rely on a solid and coherent metapsychology. This double debunking of received notions may not only enlarge the respective frames of reference of both the therapeutic and the academic communities; it may also allow them to find a common denominator in a metapsychology that has derived its "scientific" status from the unexpected realm of the humanities.

I would like to end this overview to the series as a whole with a word of warning and a word of reassurance. One of the great difficulties for an American analyst trying to figure out the Lacanian "genre" is the way these clinical theorists explain their theoretical point of view as if it were coming straight from Freud. Yet Lacan's Freud and the American Freud are far from being transparent to each other. Lacan dismantled the Freudian corpus and rebuilt it on entirely new foundations, so that the new edifice no longer resembled the old. At the same time he always downplayed, with a certain *coquetterie*, his position as a theory builder, because he was intent on proving that he had remained, despite all odds, true to Freud's deepest insights. Since Lacan was very insistent on keeping Freudian concepts as the raw material of his theory, Lacanian analysts of the second generation have followed in their master's footsteps and have continued to read Freud scrupulously in order to expand, with new insights, this large structure that had been laid out. Moreover, complicated historical circumstances have fostered their isolation, so that their acquaintance with recent psychoanalytic developments outside of France has been limited. Lacan's critical views on ego psychology and selected aspects of object relations theory have continued to inform their vision of American psychoanalysis and have left them unaware that certain of their misgivings about these schools of thought are shared by some of their colleagues in the United States. This apparently undying allegiance to Freud, therefore, does not necessarily mean that Lacanians have not moved beyond him, but rather that their approach is different from that of their American counterparts. While the latter often tend to situate their work as a reaction to Freud, the Lacanian strategy always consists in rescuing Freud's insights and resituating them in a context free of biological determinism.

Second, I want to repeat that the expository style of the books of this series bears no resemblance to Lacan's own writings. Lacan felt that Freud's clarity and didactic talent had ultimately led to distortions and oversimplifications, so that his own notoriously "impossible" style was meant to serve as a metaphor for the difficulty of listening to the unconscious. Cracking his difficult writings involves not only the intellectual effort of readers but also their unconscious processes; comprehension will dawn as reader-analysts recognize in their own work what was expressed in sibylline fashion in the text. Some of Lacan's followers continued this tradition, fearing that clear exposition would leave no room for the active participation of the reader. Others felt strongly that although Lacan's point was well taken it was not necessary to prolong indefinitely an ideology of obscurantism liable to fall into the same traps as the ones Lacan was denouncing in the first place. Such a conviction was precisely what made this series, The Lacanian Clinical Field, possible.

—Judith Feher-Gurewich

Introduction

STEVEN L. ABLON, M.D.

It was with uncertainty and curiosity that I decided to read Catherine Mathelin's *Lacanian Psychotherapy with Children: The Broken Piano*. I had only a limited knowledge of Lacanian psychoanalysis and no experience of Lacanian analysis with children. Most likely this book is one of the first presentations in English of Lacanian child analysis. I have found different points of view about analysis, especially different clinical perspectives, to be extremely valuable. These points of view underscore commonalities and, more importantly, raise exciting ideas and questions. The book exceeded my expectations in just the way Mathelin hoped: "[analysts] must be alert to remaining alive and creative, ready to let themselves be surprised, educated, unsettled" (p. 17).

The book begins with "The First Meeting with the Analyst, Thirty Years Later." Like an overture, this chapter underscores the main themes. A central point of view, quoted from Françoise Dolto (1965), is that "[i]t is the child who unconsciously bears the burden of the tensions and disturbances in the unconscious psychosexual dynamics of the parents" (p. 3). This is powerfully elaborated: "What the parents are unable to express . . . is expressed through their child. Thus the child may not suffer even when the realities of his life seem to us to be distressing: what hurts is in another register" (p. 5). Mathelin's descriptions of consultations to fourteen children and families illustrate this point of view in a compelling way. These brief clinical presentations are much like Winnicott's classic accounts of therapeutic consultations with children. Mathelin's clinical skill and evocative powers as a writer make these case examples richly detailed and moving. There is much to be learned from these "distinctive features of the encounter with the analyst, a privileged, 'magic' moment unlike any other, a time when masks can fall and a truth can arrive" (p. 6). I learned from 9-year-old Félicien, whose psychologist mother was worried about what she called an "Oedipal problem"; from 7-year-old Arthur, whose violence echoed his mother's fantasies ("am I a murderer?"); and from 11-year-old Lolita, "the abnormal child," who was helped to tell her mother, "'Y' see, the problem is that I scare Mom too much'" (p. 62). Regarding adult and child analysis, Mathelin makes the crucial point that

> the stakes are the same for children and adults, and that the analyst cannot help taking risks. But if, with adults, the analyst can sometimes—mistakenly—feel protected by the frame, in child analysis the inventiveness that is required makes the work more dangerous. It is impossible to fool children, who know what "telling the truth" means. [p. 13]

Mathelin's consultations are valuable correctives to the current emphasis on children's problems being the result of childrearing, biology, or cognitive and learning difficulties: "[I]t is easier to believe that childrearing can be corrected by following recipes—even those based on psychoanalytic theory—than to believe that children can be made ill by something outside our control, something mysterious, terrifying, that lies beyond us: the unconscious" (p. 6). Mathelin emphasizes that "the psychoanalyst's role goes beyond giving treatment and selfishly accumulating knowledge; rooted in his experience of human suffering, it extends beyond his office to his activities in daily life" (p. 12). A valuable aspect of this book is the way it underscores the enormous value of informed teamwork between pediatrician and analyst. This is often an area that American child analysts have abandoned, leaving it to consultation psychiatrists. The strength of this book resides in the clinical elaboration. We learn about a 9-year-old girl, Carla, and the importance of both the pediatrician and the analyst listening to her heart. There is also the case of Anna, where "[t]he doctor's detailed answers to the girl's questions, her wish to keep her alive—that is, to do her job as a doctor—enabled Anna to tolerate the analytic situation" (p. 78). Most powerful is the situation of Alexandre, or "the broken piano," a physically disabled 10-year-old boy who learned that both his analyst and his pediatrician "were committed to the same project of offering him different spaces in which he could, if he chose, 'manage' his illness and examine his desire" (p. 80).

In the section entitled "From the First Session to the Analytic Treatment," Mathelin, in a beautifully written, engaging way, presents the clinical work that brings three children from consultation to analysis. This is also a testimony to Susan Fairfield's excellent translation. Here is an example of Mathelin's descriptions:

> [The parents] recounted a history that was smooth and tranquil, without suffering, just like the face of Alice, who lis-

tened, without blinking an eye, to a narrative as orderly as the ribbons in her hair, as the pleats in the little pink dress spread out around the child-doll.

And yet sometimes Alice would have terrible tantrums, would scream, bite, hit her head against the wall or the floor, rupturing the silence of the house. [p. 109]

The children Mathelin describes are in the autistic realm. Although her technical approaches are valuable in thinking about autistic children, they are clearly applicable to all analytic work with adults and children. For example, regarding the drawings, whose inclusion is an invaluable dimension of the book, Mathelin writes:

It is clear that a child's drawing is to be interpreted the same way as the discourse of an adult, but—as is also the case with adults—always in an interrogative mode, as if suggesting a working hypothesis while remaining open to being questioned and surprised. It is always the child who instructs. As Freud said, we have to be wary of presuppositions and prejudices. The only thing we have to go on in the sessions, and especially when we make interpretations, is what the patient, adult or child, has brought in. It is important to avoid being drawn into interpretative frenzies concerning these drawings, and, with drawings as with dreams, to stay close to the patient's associations. [p. 96]

This book, steeped in the importance and tradition of words, of the signifier and the signified, presents a paradox. On the one hand, the value of talking from the heart to children, even to infants, is cogently supported. At the same time, the importance of non-verbal communications such as facial expressions and other aspects of body language is barely mentioned. Mathelin seems aware of these struggles:

There are many questions that, of course, [remain] unanswered and that we must not try to answer by forcing them into a theoretical framework; this is always detrimental to an analysis, since clinical practice, contrary to what one too often hears, is not intended to illustrate theory. Theory, for its part, cannot explain everything, but it provides guidelines for treatment so that clinical work is not haphazard. [p. 104]

In this book words are spoken with courage and authority, and from a place of intuition:

Alice had turned back towards me like an automaton. She looked out the window over my shoulder but seemed to see nothing there. She kept on repeating, "It's raining? It's raining?" I said, "It's sunny out, but maybe it's raining in Alice's heart? Maybe Alice would like to know if it's also raining in her mommy's heart?" Alice met my gaze for the first time. She rushed over to her mother's handbag and, in one movement, came back and emptied it violently at my feet. Then she flung herself towards her mother and pressed her head against the woman's stomach. [p. 109]

Another powerful example of surefooted intuition is the following:

Jeremy looked at me in surprise, his eyes a transparent blue. He began to smile and went to the desk to take felt-tip pens and paper. "Wait," he said. "I'll tell you about the fire." He took a pen in his hand and began to cry: "No, no, Jeremy can't draw." He held out the pen: "You do it, you do it."
    I took the pen and asked him what he wanted me to draw. This was the first time a child had asked me to draw for him, but in Jeremy's tears I had understood that I had to

accept a task that at this time he found impossible. It was a question not of drawing for him but of letting him make use of my drawings. His anxiety was too great, and I had to go along with him. [pp. 130–131]

The three cases that move into analysis are riveting, like this excerpt from the treatment of 7-year-old Alice:

Alice then went crazy. She bit herself, hit her head against the wall, threw herself at me and scratched me, tore at her hair and mine. I took her hands firmly in my own and spoke to her over and over about her panic, about the horror she was experiencing, about her fragmented body and the volcano inside her head that was causing her so much pain. I told her that I would help her to contain her fears and her panic; just as I was holding her hands, I would help her to understand. She gradually calmed down, and the storm was over, leaving both of us exhausted. [p. 110]

The importance of words is clear in Mathelin's quote from Lacan:

In this very special case, we see, embodied there, this function of language, we touch on it in its most reduced form, reduced down to a word whose meaning and significance for the child we are not even able to define, but which nonetheless ties him to the community of mankind. [p. 125]

There are many unforgettable aspects of Mathelin's dialogues with children, such as: "But after twelve years of analysis, one morning when she was quite sad, Alice, who did not know sadness, said to me: "Alice doesn't like you, Mathelin. You've made her too unhappy. Now Alice will never be able to be the way she used to be" (p. 128). Or when Mathelin first met 8-year-old Jeremy in her courtyard, threatening everyone, breaking tiles, and she found a way for him to find himself. Mathelin's courage is inspiring. Her view of the therapeutic value of play is also something I have come to learn from my child patients:

> Each advance in this child's treatment seemed to be connected, not to interpretations, which were apparently useless, but instead to the staging of what was going on in his interior theater, his extraordinary fantasy life. The same play, each time it was repeated in every session, was no doubt what finally enabled his story to be inscribed and to take on meaning. It took years to play out the theme of the clown and the man, to clarify the meaning of the sheet of glass that had to be broken through in order to escape from the world of the dead, and to put a stop to the metonymic sliding of ice, water, and mirror in which Jeremy had become lost. He staged his story (for it is not the analyst who is the producer of the drama), anchoring himself in the transference session after session so as to be able to write his theory, his own myth. [pp. 140–141]

I think it is time for me to stop. There is more, much more, including a review and critique of infancy research and a discussion of the analyst at work on a neonatal unit. I hope my comments help you to find Mathelin and her extraordinary book. In conclusion, I say read this book, take its text like the unconscious, and, as Mathelin writes, remember that

> [t]he analyst, following Freud's recommendation, is without prejudice and without preconceived ideas, available, open to the other and to the unconscious. If theory guides

us, it is only so that we may better listen to our analysands. Each child has his own theory, and it is from him that we get it. The analyst has no guarantees as he practices, and the unconscious, in its cunning, is not a potluck supper. Are we afraid of finding there a wine other than the one we brought? [p. 18]

Part I

The First Meeting with the Analyst

The First Meeting with the Analyst, Thirty Years Later

> *Father:* But Mommy bathes you. Are you afraid she'll drop you in the water?
>
> *Hans:* I'm afraid she'll let go and my head will fall in the water.
>
> *Father:* But you know Mommy loves you and wouldn't let go of you.
>
> *Hans:* I just thought it.
>
> —Herbert Graf, age 4, Freud's "Little Hans"

Nearly thirty years ago Maud Mannoni (1965) published a book with a Foreword by Françoise Dolto, *Le Premier Rendez-vous avec le psychanalyste* (*The First Meeting with the Analyst*). The book was also a first encounter with the analyst for the public at large, who discovered in it a new style, a new approach to child analysis. The change in tone was apparent right from the Foreword, in which Dolto emphasized the uniqueness of analytic work, the need for preventive treatment in the psychology of family relations, and—even more revolutionary—the link between the parents' unconscious and that of the child: "It is the child who unconsciously bears the burden of the tensions and the disturbances in the unconscious psychosexual dynamics of the parents" (pp. 13–14).

This overturning of traditional notions in child analysis had begun a year earlier, with the appearance of Mannoni's (1964)

L'Enfant arriéré et sa mère (*The Retarded Child and his Mother*). For the very first time, it was recognized that the child could be its parents' symptom. These findings subsequently informed the clinical and theoretical work not only of Mannoni, but also of Françoise Dolto, who, as Alain Vanier (1993a) put it, reinvented child psychoanalysis in France. They established guidelines for an entire generation of analysts.

The surprise effect was all the stronger because, since the time of Freud, the connection between children's problems and those of their parents had not received special attention in psychoanalytic conferences or publications. Although, in the case of Little Hans, Freud (1909) had broached the idea of a continuity between the parents' fantasies and the son's phobia, he did not go into detail. From the time of his discovery of the Oedipus complex and throughout his case histories, Freud often let it be understood that certain sexual fantasies in parents affected the way this complex was established in their children (as, for example, in the case of the homosexual girl [1920]), but these hints were not developed further.

Anna Freud, daughter of the father of psychoanalysis and placed in charge of child analysis (imagine the complexity of the problem this created!), stressed parental errors in upbringing that "neuroticized" their children. The issue of fantasy was not uppermost in her mind. In contrast, Melanie Klein (e.g., 1961) held that fantasy life was central, since every infant has to deal with fantasmatic activity linked to the life instinct and the death instinct. But, for Klein, these are the child's own fantasies. She seems to have regarded and studied the baby apart from the context of his family. Every newborn, according to her, is in the grip of distressing fantasies—his family history has little to do with them and his upbringing still less. Whatever his childhood is like, whatever his parents think or do, the baby's fantasies are more or less the same: self-enclosed, out of touch with the fantasy of the other, formed early on as a result of various introjections of archaic or part objects, such as the father's penis penetrating the mother's womb. The child's destructive impulses, his greed, and his wish for exclusive love reflect the lasting influence of these initial fantasies. Because, according to Klein, all children must deal with these dramas, analysis is of help in addressing the problems of normal children, not just in cases of obvious disturbance or developmental deficiency.

Klein occasionally speaks of outside events that can disturb the baby's fantasy system, but she views them only as reality elements to be located on the "historical" side of the child's history. Analytic treatment is called for simply because the child is suffering; this suffering may have been aggravated or mitigated by his life history.

For Dolto (1982), the situation is entirely different. What the parents are unable to express, she says, is expressed through their child. Thus the child may not suffer even when the realities of his life seem to us to be distressing: what hurts is in another register. For Dolto, the historical fact, though it must be taken into consideration, remains secondary. The history in question has nothing to do with facts.

How could this shift have occurred? Mannoni and Dolto worked during an extraordinarily rich and fertile time of new ideas, those of Lacan's "return to Freud." These were years of immersion in the "signifier," in ascertaining "the desire of the Other," in the whirlwind of great discoveries. Dolto had been in analysis with Laforgue, who as early as 1940 was speaking of family neurosis; Mannoni, already an accredited analyst in the International Psychoanalytic Association, chose to undertake both a segment of analysis with Lacan, who had written a paper on family complexes in 1938, and supervision with Winnicott, whose concern to understand the child together with the parents is well known.

It was in this atmosphere of theoretical revision that Mannoni and Dolto provided a definitive new ethic and orientation for child psychoanalysis. In order to understand what was happening in this period, let us look at the chronology:

<u>May 1964:</u> Maud Mannoni publishes *The Backward Child and His Mother*. Her ideas are found shocking:

> The mother–child relation is established through a distorting lens. The child does not know that he is being called upon to play a role in order to satisfy his mother's unconscious wishes. . . . Unknown to him, he is in a sense being "ravished" in the desire of the mother. [p. 63]

Public opinion is outraged; it is easier to believe that childrearing can be corrected by following recipes—even those based on psychoanalytic theory—than to believe that children can be made ill by something outside our control, something mysterious, terrifying, that lies beyond us: the unconscious.

<u>1965:</u> Mannoni publishes her study of the first meeting with the analyst, with a Foreword by Françoise Dolto. Various clinical examples emphasize the distinctive features of the encounter with the analyst, a privileged, "magic" moment unlike any other, a time when masks can fall and a truth can arrive.

The meeting with the analyst involves an encounter, through the other, with one's own lie.

Neither a physician nor a psychologist nor an educator, the analyst is "severed" from the pleasure of responding to the patient's demand. No prescriptions, advice, or corrective exercises are provided, but instead a different illumination, thanks to which the child's demand and the complexity of its desire come to the foreground. The subtitle of this book is *The Child Encounters Himself*. For what is important is to give back to the child what belongs to him so that he does not have to carry his parents' baggage, so that he can continue his growth along his own path in what Dolto calls the true spirit of his sex. The child apprehends everything that is left unsaid; his symptom is his parents' lie. In her Foreword, constantly attentive to the respect we owe not only to the child but also to the parents, Dolto explains that the parents are no more guilty than a driver who causes an accident when his car gets a flat tire or is hit by another vehicle; borrowing a phrase from Ezekiel 18:2, she says that the parents have eaten sour grapes and the children's teeth are set on edge. Parents and their young children are dynamically linked by unconscious libidinal resonances. As Freud notes with reference to Little Hans, the mother's position is not easy. She appears only as the figure of destiny.

To give the child back his creativity, his freedom to think and to grow, to view the parents otherwise than as guilty: is this not an ethical concern? Let us recall that Dolto ends her Foreword by setting forth for the first time a reference to the Declaration of the Rights of the Child.

1967: In the year she publishes *L'Enfant, sa 'maladie' et les autres* (*The Child, His "Illness" and the Others*), Mannoni organizes workshops on infantile psychoses in Paris. A paper by Winnicott is read, Lacan takes part, Ronald Laing and the "antipsychiatrists" are invited, and Dolto presents "the case of Dominique" for the first time. These few days are a major event and highlight the completely new direction in which child analysis is moving. From this time on it was no longer possible to view the child entirely apart from the family. Nor was it possible to view child analysis as a "minor art," or infantile psychosis as a contraindication to psychoanalytic treatment.

1969: Françoise Dolto participates, under the name of Doctor X, in broadcasts on the station Europe No. 1. In her responses to listeners' questions, she emphasizes the importance of the paternal function and of the symbolic* and denounces the machinations of family secrecy. She explains how things left unsaid, relegated to silence, can create things permanently silenced—"murdered"—inside the child, and how these appear in the form of symptoms.

September 1969: Mannoni, with the support of Lacan and Robert Lefort, establishes the Experimental School in Bonneuil-sur-Marne.

------

*The Name of the Father (*le nom du père*) or Paternal Metaphor can be heard as both the no/*non* of the father and his name/*nom*. This pun contains the two dimensions of what Lacan understands to be symbolic castration: the negative side that enforces the prohibition of incest ("No," says the father, "you may not be your mother's phallus, the exclusive object of her desire") and the positive side, the child's inscription in the generational order (as the son or daughter of a father and a mother), which locates the child in the social world, the realm of language. Lacan's expression "paternal metaphor" not only refers to the double meaning of the *non/nom* but also points toward language *per se* as a metaphor for what has been irreversibly lost when the child becomes a speaking subject. In speaking, the subject does not know that he or she is symbolizing, through language, the object of his or her primordial yearning. For Lacan, then, castration is not merely the fear of losing or missing the penis. It is a symbolic operation that cuts the imaginary bond between mother and child and grants the boy or the girl the ability to symbolize this loss through words. Therefore, the fear of losing the penis or the frustration at not having it is grounded not in our "anatomical destiny" but in the dynamics at work within the intersubjective realm in which mother, father, and child are inscribed.

The symbolic order is the order of language and culture, the synchronic structure in which the child is inscribed, unknowingly, through the workings of the prohibition of incest (paternal metaphor). This concept of the symbolic was first proposed by the structural anthropologist Lévi-Strauss, who demonstrated how the permutations at work in the elementary structures of

The new ideas, as if echoing the rumblings of May 1968, shake the armchairs in which the analysts of the time are comfortably ensconced. Nothing will be as it was before: parents will judge themselves in new ways, pediatricians will listen to children with a different ear, social workers and remedial therapists will call into question the concepts of adjustment and rehabilitation. Analysts, obliged to take another look at psychoanalysis, will have to rethink questions about the child's demand and his suffering.

The message was clearly heard by specialists in child development. But this was thirty years ago, and whenever there is some small movement, whenever the unconscious is opened up a bit, a countermove is immediately made. Comfort must be

---

kinship not only establish the prohibition of incest as the law that transforms nature into culture, but also reveal that language and culture are both shaped by a symbolic system operating on an unconscious level. Lacan applied some of Lévi-Strauss' findings to the psychoanalytic field and went on to demonstrate how the child's submission to the prohibition of incest is concomitant with his or her entrance into language. He called upon the findings of structural linguistics in order to explain the complex relation between oedipal dynamics and language, using Freud's (1920) famous example of the *fort/da* game and Roman Jakobson's (1971) phonology to illustrate the way in which the acquisition of language goes hand in hand with the process of primal repression. Jakobson showed that every language can be structurally reduced to twelve pairs of distinct vocal, physiological contrasts that he called bipolar phonematic oppositions. An example would be the opposition *o/a* in German. Therefore, when Freud's grandson was able to say *fort/da* to symbolize his mother's leaving and returning, he had at that point already assimilated unknowingly the "differential features" characteristic of the German language. In expressing joyfully, through words, his ability to control a loss, the child in this paradigmatic anecdote at the same time repressed the cause of his sadness, and his unconscious came into being. From this moment on in development, the unconscious becomes the repository of all the phonematic traces related to subsequent experiences of loss or lack. [JFG]

restored at any cost—that is, at the cost of avoiding psychoanalysis. This process, the same every time, consists in swallowing, and preferably digesting, the monster that is getting in the way; not in rejecting it, which might only make it stronger, but in annexing it smoothly, making it one's own, appropriating it.

Today every institution comes equipped with psychoanalysts; it is impossible to function without hiring on at least one.[1] But what we most often find is that the analyst is "neutralized" there. He is decorative, to be sure, but everything is organized so as either to put him on the sidelines or to make him omnipresent, which in its own way prevents any analytic work from being done. Analysts work in outpatient clinics; in internships and externships; and in psychiatry, where patients are no longer hospitalized for schizophrenia but for foreclosure of the Name of the Father[*] (though the only thing that has changed is the way the chart is written up!); and also on medical units; in pediatrics; and sometimes even in schools.

Psychologists with analytic training are hired by both public and private schools, not only to organize discussion groups with students but also to meet with parents whose children have what are now called "learning disabilities": What becomes of the demand in this organized and more or less compulsory "unblocking" of the student? By being everywhere, doesn't psychoanalysis risk being nowhere? The possibilities for drifting out of control must not be ignored. Will the child in the year 2000 be monitored by analytic theories that no longer bear any resemblance to the Freudian discovery?

---

1. We may recall that at Bonneuil Mannoni keeps analytic treatment separate from the institution and that Dolto did not think that psychoanalysis was possible in an institutional setting.

[*]Foreclosure of the Name of the Father refers to the failure of the symbolic function and is associated with psychotic states. [JFG]

A pediatrician with no analytic training told me how he had come to offer his patients, who were getting tired of antibiotics, interpretations he had carefully written down on index cards after a conscientious reading of Françoise Dolto. A speech therapist recently came to ask me to take her on as a supervisee because, she said, she was "working with the Oedipus complexes" of her young clients and did not want to make incorrect interpretations.

As for analysts, don't they find parents handing over to them responsibility for their children's upbringing? "*You* take care of him," one father told me. "*You* won't mess him up as much as we would. Anyway, I feel fine about coming to see you; I've read that analysts don't talk, and so you won't ask me any questions." Dominique Guyomard (1992) described how she had been seen in consultation by a father who said to her, while taking out his checkbook with an expansive gesture, "Ask any price you want. My son doesn't talk. So do whatever you want as long as you make him talk, and then let's not talk about it any more."

Television shows, advice given over the radio, more or less serious articles in magazines with a wide circulation: Doesn't this hijacked psychoanalysis risk losing all the subversive power that characterizes it? And yet, isn't it essential that we be able to speak in psychoanalytic terms? Dolto was convinced that this is the case. She urged in all possible ways a different understanding of childhood, and her voice was indeed heard. At the last general meeting of the Association for Archives and Documentation on Françoise Dolto, Alain Vanier said of her that she caused as much of a revolution in today's world as Pasteur did in his time.

To be sure, we have not yet taken the measure of the upheaval in our society caused by Dolto's contributions, and its true importance will take time to recognize. But if we just think of the way a modern child spends his day, we can appreciate her impact on his relations with his parents when he gets up in the morning and on how he is welcomed at his school, which, if not actually called Françoise Dolto Daycare Center or Dolto Junior High, will at least have on its medical or teaching staff a good many people who have read her work and taken it into account. And his visits to the pediatrician will be different, provided that the doctor has come to know, through reading, television, or radio, of Dolto's intense respect for children. And, in the child's bedtime ritual at night, his parents will perhaps be more attentive to the anxiety of their little person, more available to talk to him and listen to him. In *La Difficulté de vivre* (*The Difficulty of Living*) Dolto (1982) said that, for her, the psychoanalyst's role goes beyond giving treatment and self-ishly accumulating knowledge; rooted in his experience of human suffering, it extends beyond his office to his activities in daily life.

On the societal level, her message was heard. Matters are a bit more complicated with regard to psychoanalysis itself. "Dolto effects" on patients and analysts are not always positive. Ready-made solutions and recipes come at a brisk pace, advice abounds, and children are sometimes overwhelmed by the sheer amount of goodwill, well intentioned but inane, that comes their way. Dolto knew this. When we spoke of it, one summer evening in 1983, she said with a smile:

> Yes, they'll do a Dolto, which goes to show that they don't understand anything about the unconscious. They'll be off the mark, but that's inevitable, and it's still worth it if I can get across what I have to say. It's like when you really want a color to be vivid. If you turn the paint can upside down, there'll be all kinds of spattering that you don't want, but it's

up to you, the analysts of today, to clear things up so that
little by little the spatters will disappear. What's important
is that the color be there in the center of the picture.

Françoise Dolto left her mark, her color, well beyond her
work as an analyst. What is most deserving of attention in her
work is, as usual, what is least discussed. Although she accepted
the role of good grandmother to psychoanalysis in order to con-
vey her message, she was also capable of great violence in interpretation and great exactitude in the way she went about things.
What is in danger of being smoothed over is this extraordinarily subversive and disturbing aspect of her achievement.

If we read between the lines, we most often find her to be
rigorously Freudian, presenting an image of the child that is by
no means reassuring. Faced with this child, the adult she describes and the psychoanalyst have good reason to examine and
question themselves. In her lectures, she would often reply to
analysts who persisted in asking for her expert advice: "Do stop
asking me these stupid questions; I don't have ready-made answers! You have an unconscious just as I do, so why don't you
listen to it?" Her orientation was not, as her detractors would
have it, towards pedagogy but towards psychoanalysis.

She constantly pointed out the extreme difficulty of child
psychoanalysis, which, she believed, required a thorough famil-
iarity with the unconscious. There is no question of this being a
gentler or "lighter" analysis, or a subspecialty within the field.
She warned psychiatrists and psychologists with no analytic
training against the risk they themselves ran if they undertook
to practice analysis with children. Like Maud Mannoni (1967),
who states right at the beginning of *The Child, His "Illness," and
the Others* that child analysis is analysis, Dolto insisted that the
stakes are the same for children and adults, and that the analyst

cannot help taking risks. But if, with adults, the analyst can sometimes—mistakenly—feel protected by the frame, in child analysis
the inventiveness that is required makes the work more dangerous. It is impossible to fool children, who know what "telling
the truth" means.

The words that Françoise Dolto asked to have engraved on
her tombstone sum up her analytic approach: "Do not be afraid."
And indeed we should not be afraid, if only in order to be able
to combat the undesirable effects of media coverage and to maintain at all costs the message and the rigor that she imparted to
us so that we may transmit them in our turn.

In these same years, Mannoni's position with regard to the
media was more subdued; nevertheless, she lent her "color" in
a solid and fundamental way to the professional world of psychoanalysis and to institutions. She, too, was unable to prevent
a certain drifting and sterile imitating of her ideas. The impact
of the founding of the Bonneuil School, in the turmoil of the years
around 1968, was so great that many establishments today claim
to be putting her theories into practice. When "doing it the
Bonneuil way" becomes a recipe, the results will inevitably be
disastrous; theory then serves as a barrier against the unconscious. But here, too, don't we have to pass on the message and
show that an institution can function otherwise than along traditional psychiatric lines?

Today there are consultations that no longer include children, on the grounds that it is enough to see the parents alone
to cure the child of his symptoms. But whoever takes the trouble
to read Maud Mannoni will never accept such a deviation. The
interest and the respect that she shows for the child in his own
right do not allow us to imagine that he could be excluded from
a psychoanalytic consultation, since it is he who carries the symptom and is suffering. The symptom belongs both to the child and

to the parents, and it is in this middle ground that we have to work.

Should Mannoni not have written *The Backward Child and His Mother,* so as to avoid distortion of her thinking? Of course not. But this just goes to show that analysts of today cannot rest on the laurels of an older generation's discoveries. We must continue to redefine, moment by moment, what psychoanalysis is and especially what it is not. In each session with a child, we must reinvent the psychoanalyst's working instrument, not just in accordance with theoretical guidelines but in accordance with our own unconscious. Perhaps what should be emphasized above all else is the importance of an ethic, if we want it to be possible for the generation of analysts twenty years from now to write: "The First Meeting with the Analyst, Fifty Years Later."

As far as families are concerned, the dissemination of psychoanalytic theory has had its effects. Can patients, informed as they are by the media, still be surprised at the first interview? The remarks of several clever mothers confirm our worst fears.

<u>Pierre's Mother</u>. She had made an appointment for her son, but she came alone, explaining:

> I told Pierre and his father that there was no point their coming. I know that the problem lies with me. Besides, everyone knows that when an 8-year-old is having difficulties, look for what's wrong with the mother. Pierre has always been asthmatic, but it's getting worse right now. The symptom is definitely a sign of my anxiety—by the way, while we're talking about signs, I'm an Aquarius with a Sagittarius ascendant, so just imagine! I don't have to spell it out; I'm sure you understand!

The only thing I understood was that Pierre was suffocating. "That's normal," his mother said ironically. "*I did everything* for him." He was on maximum doses of sedatives and broncho-dilators and was at risk of death. Once again the time, the space, in which he could have spoken had been usurped. I made an appointment for Pierre, but he never showed up.

Sylvie. She was alone on the other side of the door at the time of her first interview with the analyst. She was 7 years old. I had her come into my office, and she explained that her parents had wanted her to come by herself. "Making peepee in bed," they had told her, "is your problem. Sort it out by telling the lady about it; you're the one who has to talk, not us. We'll pick you up outside the building in an hour." Sylvie said that she didn't understand why she was there; she was perfectly well. The very infrequent bedwetting that bothered her parents (since they had set up the appointment) didn't bother her. She didn't want to come back. When she left I gave her an appointment time for her parents; they never came.

François. When he arrived alone in my office for the first time, he lay down on the couch. When I expressed surprise, he said, "Well, isn't that what psychoanalysis is supposed to be? Even though I'm 9, I have to talk to you about my problems and my dreams. I saw that on TV." It took many sessions before François could regain the child's position that was his and our work could finally get underway.

These three initial sessions are typical of the difficulty, one might even say the perversity, of the traps we have to avoid nowadays in order to restore an analytic dimension to interviews that are so often preprogrammed. These children and their parents remind me of actors going through the performance of a familiar play. Widespread media attention to psychoanalysis has made the element of surprise increasingly rare, as if the point were to make sure there would not be any, that nothing would emerge—no revelation, no return of the repressed. In former times patients were caught off guard at the first meeting with an analyst. Today they think they know what they are getting into. But while there are certainly more resistances, and our work is therefore all the more difficult, in a way things are still the same as they were thirty years ago, because families never find the analysis to be just what they expected. Let us hope that the same is true of the analysts, who must be alert to remaining alive and creative, ready to let themselves be surprised, educated, unsettled.

If theory is present, it is so only as an accompaniment to our work, as a reference point or guardrail, but it never blocks the risk of an encounter. In no case should it lead us to pin a ready-made answer or idea on the history of a child and his family. No two people are alike; each new meeting is a "first time." Winnicott (1971a) nicely summed up the role of theory when, in the Introduction to *Therapeutic Consultations in Child Psychiatry*, he said that, as he explored a new case, his only companion was the theory that had become a part of him and so did not have to be referred to deliberately.

When we listen to a child we must learn, and the only way to do this is to admit that we don't know. Or perhaps to admit that our knowledge, having become a part of us, cannot turn us into magicians or miracle workers. The analyst's attitude must be one of humility. Omnipotence will be quickly denounced by the child, and the silent, absent analyst who thinks he is maintaining his "role" will be mercilessly flushed out of his ridiculous hiding place by his little patient.

We have to work with all our faults. Winnicott (1971a) says that he interprets mainly to let the patient know the limits of what the analyst understands. Every blunder impedes the possibility of authentic presence, of creation, of "full speech" in Lacan's (1953–1954) sense: "Full speech is speech which performs. . . . One of the subjects finds himself, afterwards, other than he was before" (p. 107). The analyst, following Freud's recommendation, is without prejudice and without preconceived ideas, available, open to the other and to the unconscious. If theory guides us, it is only so that we may better listen to our analysands. Each child has his own theory, and it is from him that we get it. The analyst has no guarantees as he practices, and the unconscious, in its cunning, is not a potluck supper. Are we afraid of finding there a wine other than the one we brought?

1

Félicien and the "Intellectual Women"[1]

Félicien's mother arranged an appointment on the advice of her own mother, a psychologist. Félicien had just celebrated his ninth birthday. He was in good health and did well in school, but his mother was very anxious about him. She said:

> There's no mystery about Félicien's difficulties. We know what the matter is; he's got an oedipal problem. His father left us when he was 18 months old. Since then we've lived on our own, and I gave all my affection to him. Recently he's had a lot of trouble leaving me in the morning to go to school. He has nightmares and usually sleeps in my bed. It's no use my saying no—as I know I should—because he sleeps there anyway. He also has migraines. I get them also, and I understood right away that it was my head that was hurting him.

---

1. Translator's note: The reference is to the title of Molière's comedy *Les Femmes Savantes*, in which the pretensions of bluestockings are mocked.

Félicien listened to his mother with a weary air, yawning. I said to him: "Félicien, your mom has said why *she's* here. Do *you* know why you came?

> *Félicien:* I dunno. [Glancing at his mother, who was frowning] Yes, I know. Mom said that I don't want to grow up, that I need a man in the house.
> *C.M.:* What do *you* think about that?
> *Félicien:* I dunno, and I don't give a fuck!

Mother got angry: "Oh no, Félicien, don't put on that act of someone who has no demand! Just this morning you refused to go to school!"

> *Félicien:* Yeah, I don't like gym. It's too cold in the stadium.
> *Mother:* Come on, you're exaggerating! You don't feel well, that's why you don't like gym!
> *Félicien:* Who cares!
> *Mother:* And the bad dreams that wake you up every night? And what about the problems with the kids at school that you never want to invite over?
> *Félicien:* That's my private life, and I don't want to talk about it! You didn't have to bring that up!
> *Mother:* That's why we came here. Here there are no secrets. Remember the time you cried and told me that you were scared that you might see your father again one day? And I spoke to you about how hard it is for you to feel that you're a boy?

I was beginning to think that the mother had forgotten my presence, when she turned to me.

Mother: So, when can you see him, so that you can talk to him about all this? His grandmother and I are clear about the fact that he has to be in therapy. A few sessions ought to be enough, don't you think?

I had no answer to this question. I had no such thought, I told Félicien and his mother. Unlike her, I didn't know what would be good for him. Nothing occurred to me, except that the mother was terribly anxious. Her relentless interpreting had made her deaf to her son and at the same time had made it impossible for me to listen to him. "Set up an appointment to talk to him," she said. But wasn't it more a matter of listening to this child? He seemed unhappy and misunderstood despite all the knowledge of his mother and grandmother. How did he experience all that? What role did his father play for him?

The mother was very surprised when I suggested another appointment for Félicien alone and made it clear right from the outset that this place was for him, that he could say anything, but that he also had a right to his secrets. By challenging his mother's assertion that there were no secrets here, I spoke of the confidentiality of the sessions: neither mother nor grandmother would be informed of what would be said. I also made it clear that nothing would be decided, nothing would be arranged, without him.

There was no way of telling in advance whether it would be possible to work with this child. How could I talk with him without repeating the kind of lullaby he had been hearing since his babyhood? It was important that I not become the supervisor of the grandmother who, it seemed, was already supervising this put-upon mother. If I were to be able to work with the mother, I would have to get her to give up the pseudo-theoretical fictions that were sustaining her resistances.

Did Félicien have a demand? After he left, I found on my desk a ten-franc coin with which he had been playing in his pocket and that he had ended up by "forgetting." Should I take what he said at face value? What was the meaning of this coin? Why suggest an appointment in spite of everything? To be sure, Félicien showed signs of anxiety and pain behind his overt refusal. It isn't always the case, when a child says, "I want to come," that it will be possible to work with him. He may be caught up in the wish not to disappoint his parents, or, even worse, in the analyst's seductiveness.

A demand takes time to develop, to be worked out. A despairing child who has lost all confidence in adults will not ask for their help, and the analyst belongs to the enemy camp. The child's suffering is a sign that he has a demand but is much too afraid to formulate it. It was only after many preliminary interviews that Félicien was able to say how unhappy he was. Winnicott (1971b) emphasized how precious this time is when he spoke of the sacred moment that can be seized or lost, strengthening or shaking the child's confidence.

The beginning of the treatment is crucial for the rest of the work. It is a privileged moment in which the transference, often present even before the first session, will take on another tonality or, alternatively, will be discouraged. In the initial sessions the parents are there to talk about the child and themselves, but during the opening phase the child is alone with the analyst. How many children are followed for years without making progress because this opening phase was skipped over? To the question, "You were seeing Mr. or Ms. X for psychotherapy?" the child says, "No." "Did you come to understand more about your life; did your therapy help you to know why you were unhappy?" "No." "So why were you there?" "Mom wanted me to go." Or "Ms. X was nice." Or "She liked children."

As if analysts were there to like children! All those years lost because Ms. X was unable to talk to the child about her profession as an analyst, about the work they could do in this place that is unlike all other places, work done in the child's name and not that of his parents. The analyst must take the time to explain the fundamental rule and the principle of confidentiality. A child is taught not to speak out in front of grownups: "Don't say that the lady is ugly"; "Don't say the cake is no good"; "Don't say that you hate your little brother." How can he understand, unless we work with him, that it is different in therapy? We must be patient: a child's time is not that of an adult, and we must respect this so that little by little, once he is alone with us, he can allow himself to speak of his suffering, or even to declare that he is not suffering, without being reprimanded by a family more or less disappointed at being deprived of sessions with the analyst. It is more structure-building for a child to say no in this situation than to be dragged to appointments during which neither he nor the analyst understands anything.

The opening phase brings up the issue of demand and desire. When Félicien became able to speak of his unhappiness in words other than those of his mother's books, and when he finally asked to understand what the "shrinks" did not understand, I was in a position to offer him a course of analytic work. We were no longer dealing with notions and concepts devoid of meaning, but with a pain so authentic that it hurt him in his body and made him want to cry out. This was a cry that could be heard here. I took the time to let him become certain of this, and then he asked to come, having finally found a space in which he was allowed to express his horror.

For it is most often horror, hatred, and death that are at issue in child analysis. In no case is it a matter of sugary generosity and devoted good will, but instead of the transference at its most violent. And we must be prepared for it. Félicien said, "Sometimes I feel like banging my head against the wall and screaming. Mom always knows why I'm unhappy and explains it to me. I don't understand what she's saying; she doesn't know it hurts inside and I can't tell her, but I want to talk about it."

The Department of Health agreement to pay the fee came through at this time, but, curiously, the mother was already beginning to think that analytic treatment was no longer really necessary. Nevertheless, she went along with Félicien's decision. I saw her together with the child about once a month.[2] She slowly gave up trying to pin her ready-made theory on Félicien's words and had to face what was unbearable about her own suffering and that of her child.

As Mannoni (1965) says, language can be a cover-up; the patient needs time to understand that his truth lies elsewhere, and it is not always easy for the analyst to restore it to him.

---

2. I never fix the timing of conjoint sessions in advance, preferring to re-evaluate it in the context of each individual family and in step with the child's demand and his progress in the treatment.

2

Aurore and Christine,
or The Child Waiting Offstage

The parents of Aurore and Christine came to see me along with their daughters after seeing a television program about child psychoanalysis. Aurore was beautiful, tall, blonde, smiling, a fairy-tale princess who resembled her name.[1] She was 7 years old. Christine, age 5, was dark and quite small; she seemed shy and more retiring. When I went to the waiting room to bring them in, I asked which of the girls had the appointment. The parents seemed amused by this question: "Christine, of course!" We went into the office with Christine. Aurore stayed in the waiting room.

I began by asking the parents, "Why were you surprised when I asked who had the appointment?"

> *Parents:* We thought you'd see it right away! Aurore is so self-assured, so joyful. She feels so good about herself. People are always worried about Christine.

---

1. Translator's note: "Aurore" means "dawn."

C.M.: What's worrisome about her?

Parents: She's small, a bit too small for her age. She's very
reserved. In school, she's doing very well according to
the teacher; she has friends, she likes to work. But as
we see it, she's very quiet. Aurore talks a lot and is always center stage. It seems to us that Christine is a bit
overwhelmed by her big sister. On TV they said that
younger children suffer when the older ones are too
self-confident, so Christine must surely be unhappy.

Christine was smiling while her parents spoke about their
concern. I could see that they were worried, but I didn't understand why. Christine didn't like to talk about what she did in
school from day to day, but that was her right. She didn't like
family gatherings and preferred to listen to her records or look
at her books. And perhaps with good reason.

She spoke perfectly well, enjoyed playing with her friends,
also liked to be by herself. She drew very well and was just start-
ing piano lessons. The parents were concerned because she spent
a lot of time practicing at the piano. Though I tried my best to
listen, I simply could not see what was bothering them.

I explained to Christine who I was and what sort of work
we could do together. Did she want something to change? Did
she feel unhappy? "Oh, no," she answered. "Everything's fine."
I mentioned that her parents had said that they were worried
because she didn't talk a lot. "That's because I don't always feel
like talking," she replied.

The parents seemed to be on the lookout for symptoms.
What symptoms? As the hour came to an end, I still didn't
understand what they wanted from me, but I understood that
Christine, for her part, wanted nothing. I suggested that the
parents come to discuss their concern with me, since it was

they who seemed to want help. Perhaps it was not Christine, but something else, that was on their minds? They agreed to another session.

We went back to the waiting room. Aurore had torn out a piece of paper from the notebook in her schoolbag and drawn a picture. When she saw me come in, she rushed over to me and gave me the drawing, saying, "It's for you! Look at it!" Something in the urgency of this little girl made me feel that I had to listen to her. I looked at the drawing. It was the sort of picture all 7-year-old girls draw: flowers, a sun, a beautiful princess with a carefully decorated gown full of sparkling jewels, gray clouds, a deep blue sky.

Among the sprinkling of flowers were a few small red mushrooms that attracted my attention, and I asked her about them:

C.M.: Oh, that's kind of odd, so many mushrooms . . . .
Aurore: Yes, they're poisonous; you know, deadly mushrooms.
C.M.: And the gray clouds up there?
Aurore (smiling): Yes, those are toxic fumes that kill people when it rains.
C.M.: And these hills on which you planted the flowers?
Aurore (still smiling): These are the lairs of the living dead. They come at night to cut people's throats and suck their blood; sometimes they smother them.

I was beginning to be afraid to ask any more questions. This drawing was like a horror film. "And the princess? Is she in danger?"

Aurore: The princess is the one who orders the other ones to kill. So she's afraid that they'll come and take revenge.

The parents looked stunned. "Aurore, how can you say things like that, such horrible things, a nice girl like you!"

I could see that something was written on the other side of the paper, so I turned it over, expecting to find her name. She had not written "Aurore" but just three letters: S. O. S.

The parents were correct in feeling that they needed a consultation, only they didn't know for whom they had come. We often find that a family's demand on behalf of one child actually concerns another. Sometimes it takes more than one session to realize this. The guilt that was devouring Aurore and her parents could be spoken of only through their "victim," who was bearing up very well. It isn't always the preferred child in a family who is in the better position.

How many times do we leave in the waiting room the child who holds the key to the enigma? The one who, waiting in the wings, watches the play without taking part, the one who, lifting the veil from the oedipal drama when the time comes, will explode everything. He will come onstage when least expected to denounce the deceit, the hoax. He will break the spell that has hypnotized the analyst fascinated by the performance. Whether through acting out, a suicide attempt, or a narcissistic collapse, the offstage child will be revealed as the one the parents carried within themselves over the years, the parents who will be devastated when they have to accept responsibility for their "real" child.

It isn't easy to discern this pattern, given the multiple demands, multiple transferences, and external interventions on the part of doctors or the school. Who is demanding what? How, in this labyrinth, can we find the red thread that will finally enable the child to come to occupy the position of subject?

3

Arthur and the Secret of the Sea Elephants

To say everything is not to tell all.

Arthur was a 7-year-old first grader whose parents came to see me on the advice of his teacher. She could not do anything with him: he was too unruly, too disobedient; he attacked other children and was extremely violent. According to the school, he was intelligent and perfectly able to keep up with the class, but his conduct was so disastrous that expulsion was being considered.

> *Parents:* It's terrible having a child like this! He can't keep still. We can't keep on hitting him—we know we shouldn't, but life at home is getting to be impossible.
> *C.M.:* What do you think, Arthur?
> *Arthur:* Sometimes I want to kill my friends, but there's nothing wrong with that.

Arthur went right for the paper and the felt-tip markers and drew while his parents were talking, one picture after another without stopping. I asked what he was making.

Arthur: This first one's a sea dragon, a really bad one. And this one's a terrible octopus that eats everything up.

Parents: It's awful. We've done everything we could, everything we were advised to do.

Father: My wife knows all about psychology. She knows what to do. For example, we never kept any secrets from him; everyone knows secrets are bad.

Arthur continued drawing: "a whale with big teeth," "sea elephants," "waves, water."

Mother: Always water—all he draws is water and animals that live in the water. This has got to represent the fetal stage. I bathe him a lot; I tell myself that maybe he has to regress to the fetal stage in order to get out of it; don't you think so?

All I thought was that Arthur seemed more and more terrified the more he drew.

Mother: Do you think children remember the time when they were fetuses?

Father: No, come on, they're too little then. Even babies aren't aware of anything.

Mother: Do you believe that babies have thoughts?

Arthur suddenly stopped drawing and looked at his mother.

C.M.: What was Arthur like as a baby?

Mother: He knows all about it, how he was. I was happy to be pregnant. No problems, a wonderful delivery just like in the films where they recommend natural childbirth. He was beautiful. I never saw such a fine baby!

Arthur began drawing again. Under the elephant he drew circles and explained: "These are eggs. Under the sea elephant there are eggs, but they're all going to die; she's going to crush them; look—smash! smash! They're squashed, broken, all ruined." Mother began to cry. Father explained: "Arthur knows the whole story. We lost a child, a boy named Etienne. We've always told Arthur everything, so he knows.

Mother: When Arthur was three, I gave birth to another little boy. At first everything was fine; the pregnancy was normal. I felt fine going into labor, but at the last moment I realized that something was very wrong. The midwife suddenly looked worried and said that I should have had a Caesarian. I could see that the people around me were becoming panicky, and I even thought they were arguing. When the baby came out he didn't cry. I was terribly worried. He needed oxygen and they took him away immediately to try to resuscitate him. I went to see him the next day and he had tubes stuck in him all over. He didn't react to anything.

Father: Arthur knows all this, so it can't be what's making him so aggressive. Maybe if we'd kept it a secret; but as it was, no problem! We told him everything.

Mother: Three days after he was born, the doctors called us in and told us that they didn't know whether he would live or die, but they thought there was a lot of brain damage and he would be abnormal, broken—yes, I remember, the brain was *broken*, that's the word they used, and here's Arthur who draws broken eggs!

Father: Look, let's not talk any more about all that. You know it makes you ill every time. Arthur knows all about it, and it's got nothing to do with him.

I asked the mother to continue.

Mother: What's so awful is that I remember very well—I don't know how to tell you this—but I said to them that if he was really broken then they had to "do something." They said, "Look, Madame, we really can't comply with a such a request." I insisted and insisted, but they wouldn't say anything. On the morning of the sixth day, when I had just come home, the phone rang and I heard a voice saying, "This is the neonatal unit. Your baby has taken a turn for the worse." We rushed to the hospital, but by the time we got there he was dead. The most awful thing is that I'll never know whether he died a natural death or if the doctors stopped the oxygen because I'd said I didn't think I was able to take care of a handicapped child. I asked them, but their answer wasn't clear. I still dream about it at night. Did I kill this child?

She wept. Arthur stopped drawing and climbed up on her lap.

Mother: He knew his little brother was dead, and nothing else. But now this drawing—do you think he understood the whole thing?

Arthur's violence, his wish to "slaughter" everyone, was an echo of his mother's fantasy: "Am I a murderer?" As if to reassure her, Arthur seemed to be telling her that her secret wasn't so terrible: "I want to kill them, but there's nothing wrong with that." Above and beyond the unsaid thing that she wanted so much to say, there was Arthur's own guilt that could only mirror his mother's in an anguish arranged by a devouring superego.

As for the father, he was terrified at the thought of intervening. His only concern was to cover up the whole matter, so that his wife would not fall into the masked depression that followed the death of her second child. His fears prevented him from helping his son. In therapy Arthur was able to separate himself from his mother's fantasy. The mother herself decided to enter treatment with a different analyst and was finally able to mourn Etienne. Arthur and his father regained their place in the family.

To say everything is not to tell all.

Nowadays keeping secrets from children is absolutely disapproved of. But if indeed it is important to speak out—to put words to events, dramas, joys—to think we are telling all is an illusion. How can we tell a child about the depression that we ourselves don't even know we are experiencing? What sort of fantasy is it that would make a mirror a pane of glass without reflection, without mystery? What do we know of desire?

Just as a child knows, or rather senses, that his mother is pregnant even before she confirms this with a test, he knows she is depressed even if she cannot talk about it. Children's knowledge extends to what their parents have repressed, to that knowledge that is unknown. Françoise Dolto often remarked that when a child is unbearable, climbs up the drapes, and breaks everything in the house, it is because he is trying to keep his mother busy, to distract her from her depression. Mother has to keep an eye on him all the time, scold him, contain him, and she has no time to think about herself. It's the poor person's electric shock.

No secrets were kept from Arthur, but he knew that his parents could not tell all.

4

Margot and the Magic Skin Eruptions

The parents of 8-year-old Margot brought her in, saying, "She doesn't feel good about herself. She's sad a lot, never happy with anything, complains all the time that she doesn't have what she wants."

At first I was astonished that this was all the parents mentioned. I could well understand that Margot didn't feel good about herself![1] Her skin was one bleeding wound, for she was covered with a spectacular case of eczema. Her arms, her hands, her neck, her eyelids were bloody. But the parents said nothing about this, continuing their psychologizing account of her attitude in school, her jealousy at the birth of a little brother three years her junior, her so-called "oedipal" difficulties involving rivalry with her mother. At last I asked:

---

1. Translator's note: "To feel good about oneself" is, in the French idiom, "to feel well in one's skin."

C.M.: And the eczema? You don't talk about it?

Father: Oh that. We don't want to talk about that; it's just the symptom. It has to be treated as a symptom and disregarded.

C.M.: You've seen a doctor?

Father: Of course not! It wouldn't make sense to treat with medicine something that's a manifestation of her psychological distress.

C.M.: What do you think, Margot?

Margot: It burns and I can't take it any more. At school there's a girl who has eczema, and she has an ointment to stop the burning. Do you know about ointments?

Mother: Sure, Margot, the easy way out, as always. Why don't you try to think about why you scratch yourself?

Margot: Because it itches.

Mother: Don't be silly. You know very well that's not the sort of thing you see a psychoanalyst about. Instead, why don't you tell her what you thought when your brother was born.

Margot: I didn't think anything. I can't stand not being able to sleep at night because of the bumps on my skin, that's all.

C.M. (to Mother): Why wouldn't one come to a psychoanalyst to talk about this?

Father: Because the symptom has to be set aside, disregarded.

C.M.: That's the second time you've spoken about disregarding. Why so?

Father: It's really annoying how people don't want to know anything about their problems! I, for one, was brave enough to be psychoanalyzed.

Mother: I think he's referring to me there. It's true, I began analysis but I found it too hard. I thought I would feel even worse if I continued, so I stopped. Ever since then, he's had it in for me. I was afraid, but I'd like for Margot to be braver.

During this time, Margot was drawing: "It's a fairy with a beautiful dress. Her castle is far away. The sun is shining high in the sky." I observed that the fairy's face was covered with red dots.

> *Margot:* Yes, those are magic bumps. See, she lost her wand. One day a storm came and broke her wand. She hasn't got one anymore, but it doesn't matter because she's got her bumps. They're magic; they have the same power that her wand used to have.
>
> *C.M.:* What would happen if she didn't have the bumps anymore?
>
> *Margot:* She wouldn't have any power, and she'd die.

How amazing the body's complicity is! Of course Margot couldn't give up her symptom. For Françoise Dolto (1982/1986), all suffering involves a demand, but suffering is not the same as a symptom: "Parents come in asking for help, but the child, because of his symptoms, is not always anxious and has no wish to understand what these disturbances mean or to get out of the difficulties in living that they reveal, let alone to talk to someone about them" (pp. 268–269).

Her father's forcing had no effect on Margot. Her burning body was what, at this time, bound her to a mother whose husband disregarded her, and this no doubt also made it impossible for Margot to be too perfect in her father's eyes, which served as a protection for her. It may also be that the magic wand broken by the birth of a little brother found its phallic replacement in the skin eruptions.

She didn't want to talk and she didn't want her eczema to disappear. All she was asking for was some ointment to soothe the flames of her desire somewhat. Why did the parents refuse her the ointment? The reasons were certainly complex, and this single session was not enough to shed light on them. Doesn't ignoring a symptom in the name of good analytic practice also mean disregarding the child who bears it and suffers from it?

Margot was protecting her mother. She knew the danger that threatened her mother and chose to let her own skin face it. She did not want to come back, and I did not give her an appointment. I suggested that the parents, who seemed to be asking for help, return to see me. But, no doubt disappointed by my attitude as well as Margot's (since I did not agree to take charge of their daughter against her will), they did not follow through. "Force her a bit," the father said. "You can't listen to what children say; they don't know what they want and they have to be put on the right track so that they'll give us what we want."

It was of course impossible to comply with injunctions like this and begin an analysis with Margot. I explained this to the child and added that if, one day, she wanted to meet with me—without being forced to by anyone, but for herself—then we could work together. In a letter to Jenny Aubry, Lacan (1969) explained, among other essential guidelines concerning the family, how the child can become the mother's object, thereby making it impossible for the mother to get in touch with her own truth. He stated that the somatic symptom is the most effective for guaranteeing this misrecognition. The symptom represents the truth, and this can be the case for the truth of a couple as well. In keeping her symptom, Margot in fantasy kept her parents. She could not do without either symptom or parents at this time. It would have been important to work with the parents, since parents' complaints must be heard if we are to pass from illness to words.[2] "He gives me an earache" or "a fever," a mother will often say. What cannot be symbolized reappears in the real.

Annie Cordié (1991) has pointed out with remarkable accuracy what is at stake regarding the mother/child relation in the language of the body:

> The psychosomatic phenomenon can be the operation of the death drives in response to an absence of inscription of the child in the desire of the Other. Conversely, it can be a response to an overinvestment in the child's body, an excess in the drive emanating from this Other. When the drive takes as its object a being who does not yet have words, who is still silent, it marks it as if with a branding iron. The organ that is invested becomes a body part in abeyance, a pound of flesh, a kind of intermediary object between mother and child, the source of shared pleasure [p. 57].[3]

That pleasure was so essential that for the time being neither Margot nor her parents could call it into question.

---

2. Translator's note: *Maux*, "pains," "illness" and *mots*, "words" are homonyms in French.

3. Translator's note: *En souffrance* means both "in abeyance; pending" and "in suffering"; *livre de chair* is both "pound of flesh" and "book of flesh."

5

Paul: How Much Does a Child Cost?

Six years old, blue eyes, hair disheveled: Paul entered my office like a hurricane. He ran, threw himself on the couch, touched everything, and wanted to see every book and open every drawer, but he did not stop to look at anything. He was everywhere at once, whirling and chattering. I caught him by the hand in mid-flight and held his gaze, explaining that in this office we had to be able to talk, that he was acting crazy, which prevented me from listening to his parents, and that his constant chattering made it impossible for me to understand what he was saying. Here in this room, I went on, words had to have space to be said, and a little boy, no matter how unhappy he was, could not come and disturb that order. "If you don't want to talk," I concluded, "you can go and wait for us in the waiting room."

He looked at me, intrigued. "Words don't do any good," he said, "and besides, I'm the one who's in charge." He then left the office, slamming the door, and went to the waiting room. His mother rushed after him: "Please, Paul, come back, darling. If you come back, Mommy will buy you a toy." And the father added: "Yes, Paul, that expensive remote-control car you wanted so much the other day." But Paul stayed in the waiting room. I tried to explain to the parents that he should not be forced to return. He respected what I had told him; he didn't want to talk, but he was waiting in another room so that we would not be prevented from talking.

The beginning of the session set the tone for what followed.

Father: We've had it. You have to cure him for us. At home it's hell. Not a day goes by that he doesn't reduce his mother to tears with his insults. And it's the same at school, a disaster. The headmaster is talking about a school for special children. He might take him on as a private pupil, but that's very expensive. We do have some money, but it's a matter of principle for me that children's education should be free. That's something society owes all of us.

Mother: But he can be nice if you give in to his whims, so we give in just to get some peace. The problem is that he wants everything and wants it right away. Nothing must bother him, nothing must be an effort for him.

C.M.: He doesn't want to pay the price?

Father: Exactly. I have to admit we spoil him a lot, but, you know, there's no question of our changing that. I was unhappy as a kid. One day I reprimanded Paul—he was about 3 at the time—and you know what happened? He began to cry, and when I saw the tears flowing silently down his cheeks, I understood that he was really unhappy. I swore to myself that I would never yell at him again. I don't want him to cry. He doesn't have to pay when we're upset. We came to see you because

we wanted you to help him be quiet without our having to have any part in it.

Mother: At one time we thought school would teach him
some discipline, but that didn't happen. Paul makes
me ill every day, and his father and I also get into
arguments because of him. My husband doesn't want
another child; he says we'd have to pay too high a price
for it.

Caught up in the problematics of *jouissance*,* where all
moves are permitted and there is no limit, Paul's parents, by
refusing to "give him castration," as Dolto used to say, were
protecting themselves and sustaining, in themselves and in their
child, the illusion of omnipotence: the moves, but not the price
to be paid.[1] Paul did not want therapy; would the parents agree
to come and talk about the impossible situation in which they
were trapped? "We can't calm him down; we can't reassure him;
we can't bawl him out. Life is hell, but, as you can see, we can't
do anything about it."

The parents agreed to another appointment for the two of
them. As I accompanied them to the door, I was surprised to

---

*For Lacan, *jouissance* is above all the prerogative of the Other. It is a
legal term, referring to the right to enjoy the usage of a thing. The *jouissance*
of the Other, therefore, is the subject's experience of being for the Other an
object of enjoyment, of use or abuse, in contrast to being the object of the
Other's desire. The experience of *jouissance* brings the subject to a point where
the boundaries between self and other become threatened. *Jouissance* is by
definition what hinders the subject's ability to symbolize the lack in the other.
(For a better understanding of the way symbolic castration separates the subject from the *jouissance* of the Other, see Gurewich 1996.) [JFG]

1. Translator's note: In this paragraph there is a pun on *coup*, "move
[in a game]" and *coût*, "price," which are homonyms.

find myself thinking that they wouldn't come. Three minutes later, the father rang the bell and said, with a big smile, "By the way, we paid you at the end of the session, and you forgot to give us the Department of Health reimbursement form." I explained that I was a private provider. "That's the last straw!" he exclaimed. "Kids have problems and we have to be the ones to pay! As if we didn't already pay enough taxes. It's a disgrace that society doesn't cover these problems. If that's the way it's going to be, we're not coming back."

Once again, there was no question of paying the price. But in order for Paul to be able to give up his omnipotence, the parents would have to give up theirs. They would have to come to terms with the fact that Paul's suffering was the suffering that occurred in their own childhood and in their marriage. They had rights, of course, but they also had duties. Isn't there a danger, in our society, that parents will think psychoanalysis is something that's coming to them?

If a child has a learning disability, parents send him to a specialist and get reimbursed; if a child is unhappy, parents send him to a psychoanalyst and likewise expect to get reimbursed. But for what? What coinage are we dealing in here? The danger we face nowadays is greater than it was twenty years ago, namely that psychoanalysis will be transformed into a kind of rehabilitation underwritten by society. There would be nothing to lose, nothing to risk. The lie would become entrenched.

To accept the price to be paid for analysis, parents have to be ready to take off the mask; as Mannoni (1965) says, they must give up the comfort of living a lie.

6

Samira: The Child as Symptom, or the Child's Symptom?

Samira was a delightful little girl of Algerian origin. Her family had been living in France for fifteen years when this 8-year-old suddenly became ill. And brutally ill. Her entire body was covered with red blotches, especially her hands and her face. Her eyes swelled up. She complained of terrible burning and itching.

Her doctors were at a loss: allergies, perhaps accompanied by asthenia and depression? She seemed to be better at night, but in the morning the blotches would reappear. The parents were advised to seek a consultation at a major Parisian hospital. They had nothing to lose, since Samira would not be allowed to go to school because of fear of contagion. The teacher could no longer stand her "color," as her mother put it.

The child was hospitalized for four days, but extensive testing yielded no evidence of allergies. So psychiatrists and psychologists were summoned to the patient's bedside. There were interviews and tests. On the fifth day of hospitalization, the verdict was rendered: "nervous allergy," no doubt caused by anxiety. Nothing serious, they said, but this was such an atypical and rare case, and its presentation was so spectacular, that Samira soon attracted a lot of attention among the hospital staff. The parents were called in, whereupon the psychologists wrote to the pediatrician that this was a religious and cultural problem; the mother was too overprotective, the father too strict.

At home, Samira was cut off from the world. Her parents lived as in the Algeria of the last century, which made contact with the school very difficult. The doctors suggested working with the mother, noting in the chart that this was a child with a "parental symptom." Getting treatment for the mother would be enough to cure the child. The father, very reluctant to let his wife go out alone, agreed to accompany her to a weekly session with the therapist at the hospital.

Two months later, Samira's condition was unchanged; it was as though she had been stung by a swarm of bees. Her teacher said that she was frightening the other children, and so she was not allowed to attend school. The pediatrician was consulted once again. Surprised that Samira was not being hospitalized, he sent her to me for my opinion.

When she arrived with her mother for the initial visit, I was able to assess the effect of her symptom on others. Everyone in the waiting room was scared and silent, and no one dared to move or to look at her. When I went to bring her in, she was smiling. Her mother reported that there was an older daughter, 19-year-old Djemila, who was at home, and a 15-year-old son, Karim, who was free of problems. The son never spoke or went out; his father would not permit it. And Samira, the youngest, had done well in school since kindergarten and had had no problems until the day when "God sent us the illness."

The father was very strict, the mother explained, wanting the family to live "like down there." In their home, religious music, traditional cuisine, prayer, and obedience were required. I asked Samira if she and I could talk alone together, and Mother returned to the waiting room.

Samira drew a lighthouse that emitted a thousand rays, saying, "It's to keep danger away." When I asked what sort of danger, she replied, "Danger is knowing things you're not supposed to know."

> C.M.: For example?
> Samira: I know things my mom doesn't know. I know how babies are made. My brother Karim makes babies with me. Ever since I was little, he sticks his hard weenie in my holes, but he says we mustn't tell anyone. My big sister, too, she says I shouldn't say anything.
> C.M.: She knows about it?
> Samira: One day she saw us. She said, "This isn't good, because you're not a virgin anymore. Don't say anything to Dad, or he'll kill you and Mom will die of grief."
> C.M.: When did you start getting sick?
> Samira: Two months ago.
> C.M.: Did something happen then?
> Samira: No. Or maybe, once, I got scared.
> C.M.: How come?
> Samira: At school, a boy climbed over the toilet wall when I was making peepee. I was afraid he'd tell everyone I wasn't a virgin anymore. I'm always afraid Dad will find out and Mom will die.

This child's dramatic story exemplifies the kind of drifting to which a certain theorization of psychoanalysis can lead. The most common risk is that the child is no longer listened to in his own right, and, likewise, the symptom is no longer considered to be the child's as well. It is as ridiculous to keep going after the symptom without trying to understand the family constellation as it is to refuse to question what pertains to the child himself. But, in Samira's case, we have to emphasize a major difference, because there was a lot more going on than fantasies.

Aren't there too often treatments in which the analyst calmly, sometimes for years, sees children victimized by sexual or physical abuse but takes no action on the grounds of benevolent neutrality or the confidentiality of the material? What effect does this complicity have on the child? What concept, what theory, justifies us in withholding the minimum respect owed to a child who, like Samira, asks to speak of the horror in her background and to be protected from it? Labeled a child who carried her parents' symptom, and therefore excluded from her mother's treatment, Samira had no way to appeal for help except by means of her lighthouse symptom that tried desperately to warn of danger. This danger was no mere fantasy!

It was in the name of psychoanalytic theory, or rather in the name of a truncated and poorly assimilated theory, that specialists had decided that Samira did not need to speak. How can we make it understood that, after twenty years of struggle to make psychoanalytic theory available in the public sector, certain ideas taken for granted nowadays have nothing to do with psychoanalysis? And how, after all these years in which we have ceaselessly tried to get specialists in other disciplines to agree that psychoanalysis is indispensable, can we make them see that it must not be regarded as holding the answer to every situation?

7

Valentin and His Lion

This 3-year-old was a superb child. Referred by his pediatrician, he came to see me with his mother and father. Mother began right away: "Valentin is doing fine, but the pediatrician is concerned because he never wants to leave me, and the pediatrician thinks that's abnormal. I've come so that you can set our minds at rest."

Valentin was seated on his mother's lap, his head pressed against her. Mother went on: "He never wants to stay with anyone but me. He adores me!" Valentin tried to extend one hand towards a basket of toys on my desk.

Mother: Don't be scared, Valentin. The toys won't bite.

Valentin immediately withdrew his hand.

C.M.: Maybe you weren't scared, Valentin?
Mother: Answer her, Valentin. The doctor won't eat you; she won't hurt you.

He began to howl.

Mother: He's afraid of everything that takes him away from
    me.

C.M.: Do you think I want to take him away from you?

Mother: I don't, but you can be sure that he does.

Valentin was indeed terrified—by me? Or wasn't it, instead,
by his mother? I turned to the father and asked what he thought
of all this.

Father: Oh, when it comes to children, I don't know a thing.
    I think it's normal when they're like that with their
    mother. Sometimes I'd like him to be different, because,
    you know, he doesn't want to play even with me.

Mother: Of course not! You scare him. You talk too loud,
    you shout.

C.M.: Valentin, are you scared of Daddy?

He nodded.

C.M.: Why?

Valentin: Dunno.

Mother: Oh yes you do, Valentin. It's because he scolds you.
    It shouldn't be that way between a father and son.

C.M.: How should it be, then?

Mother: Well, nicer, gentler, like a mother.

C.M.: What would be the point of having a father, if he did
    the same job as a mother!

Mother: I don't know; I never had a father.

This is the kind of interview it seems we've had hundreds
of times. A mother in distress, a child clinging to her because he
is afraid (as Françoise Dolto used to say, the only way not to get

bitten by a lion is to cling to its back), a father who is entirely invested in his work and has abdicated his responsibilities at home in order to be undisturbed, to have peace. This fatherless mother made no space for men or for their law. Her son was her man Friday on a desert island. Valentin was not unaware of the fact that she could not bear to have him far from her; he could not do that to her.

> *Mother:* Could you write a letter to the pediatrician, asking him to leave us alone about all this. We're really a family with no problems. No divorce, no drama—everything's fine.

Everything's fine. They would not come back despite the pediatrician, despite the magazine articles about psychoanalysis, despite the few words I said to Valentin on the doorstep:

> You see, Valentin, Mommy doesn't really know what she's protecting you from, or what she's afraid of herself, but in protecting you like this she's preventing you from growing up. Only you can make her understand that now your destiny is the same as for all other men, for your grandfathers, and for all the men who are waiting for you in order to welcome you into their clan.

As I watched them depart, I recalled an African birth ritual that Françoise Dolto had told me about. According to tradition, when a child comes into the world his mother must bend over the cradle and say: "In you, my honored son, I greet the honored male ancestors of my honored husband." For Valentin, it was this inscription in the symbolic that his mother was trying to prevent. The place left empty by her father made it impossible for her to give her son a place in her husband's lineage.

8

Violette, or the Drama of Jealousy

Violette was 6 when her parents came to see me on the advice of a pediatrician. She was shy, withdrawn, sulky, and, according to her parents, unable to make the most of herself. "She's certainly a loner," Mother said, "although it's for her that we had another child. Her little sister Marie is 18 months old."

Their pediatrician had told them what they themselves knew, that jealousy is normal at this age. They knew how to talk to their daughter, and had said everything that should be said in such cases, everything written in Françoise Dolto's books: "We'll always love you; you have the right not to love Marie and we'll never force you to, but you mustn't hurt her." It was no use: Violette hated her sister and the parents could not endure this. How was it possible, after all they'd read, and with all their knowledge (they were both teachers of "difficult" children), that Violette could not bring herself to accept Marie's birth and even wanted to choke her?

The previous week they had found little Marie suffocating as Violette, squeezing her neck hard, said to her, "I've had it!

Now you'll finally leave me alone!" "She's gone mad," the parents had thought. "Lecturing her won't do; we have to take her to an analyst." Violette listened as her parents spoke of the past eighteen months. She sulked, no doubt thinking that they were scolding her. I turned to her: "What's is it, Violette? You look very sad and angry. What do you think about what your parents have just been saying? What's going on between Marie and you? Do you want us to talk about it?"

> *Violette:* I dunno. It's normal, Daddy says, it's normal if you don't love your sister. So I don't know why they pick on me. Ever since she was born, they yell at me all the time. It's her fault. She gets on their nerves too much. When she was little, she never slept, so they were upset and took it out on me. We're at war.
>
> *C.M.:* What was Marie's birth like?
>
> *Mother:* Fine, no problems, but the pregnancy was much harder for me than when I was expecting Violette.

Violette had begun to draw a house with the shutters closed and the door barricaded, a house without flowers, without sun, a gray house. She stopped drawing in order to listen to her mother speak of the time when she was pregnant with her.

> *Mother:* I was so happy when I was expecting Violette; I wanted a little girl so much! With Marie, it wasn't the same.
>
> *Father:* That's true; you didn't want a second child.
>
> *Mother:* No, I didn't. But I was persuaded by what I read [she laughed] about how it's not good for an only child.
>
> *C.M.:* Why?

Mother: All the books say that. When a child is the only one, he gets bored, and the world revolves around him. And that's true, because the world revolved around Violette before Marie was born.

C.M.: Do you have a sister?

Mother: No, I'm an only child. My mother said that I didn't want any other children in the house, and that's why they didn't have any. It would have hurt me too much. I was 8 when my mother had a miscarriage, and I remember that they told me, "It's normal! You were so angry that it made the baby get detached." My parents adored me, and they thought that it was for the best. That way I'd stay their only daughter, the special one. Jealousy is normal. My husband and I argue all the time since Marie was born.

C.M.: Why?

Mother: I think I resent him because of what we did to Violette. He was the one who urged it on me a bit, and now I feel bad on her account. But I didn't question it after the pediatrician suggested some readings and told us again about how it's normal for an older child to be jealous. We arranged to see you so you could reassure us that everything is normal.

Father: Yes. What got us really worried was the time she wanted to strangle her. We'd like you to reassure us about that.

Mother: They do a skin test to make sure that a child is still immunized against TB. [Laughs] So people come to a psychoanalyst to be sure that the way they've explained things to a child is still protecting the child against psychological problems!

I could offer no such reassurance to Violette's parents or to her pediatrician. Violette was in danger. She felt unhappy and persecuted. All her energy was consumed by the drama she was enacting with her little sister. Most of the time, jealousy is normal in a child. He feels threatened by a baby who comes along to take his place, because he fears either identifying with the baby and sinking into a dangerous regression, or identifying with his mother, which is equally terrifying. But at other times jealousy can conceal another drama, one that goes beyond the child and belongs to the parents. Violette, her mother, her sister, her maternal grandmother: this is a story of women, a story of violence, hatred, and passion in which men scarcely have a place and are unable to calm things down. When men do not assume their symbolic function, women who "love" each other too much kill each other.

What good did it do Violette to hear reassuring interpretations, generalities offered to reduce her anxiety and silence the questions that Marie's birth raised for the parents? In such cases, the parents are like puppeteers who stage the children's hatred. Soothing words are of no avail, for a distinction must be made between pathological and normal jealousy.

A course of treatment was decided on after several sessions with Violette. It was months before the child was able to talk about her sister in a way that differed from a repetition of her mother's hate for possible usurpers. What about this maternal fantasy? The question asked of the Other in cases of jealousy concerns the imaginary place one occupies for him.[1] Hadn't

---

1. In *Birth of the Other*, Rosine and Robert Lefort (1980) note that jealousy, which is the question asked of the Other concerning what the subject is for that Other, is not the same as *invidia*, which is the question concerning the object that will satisfy the other.

Violette herself taken the place of the feared rival, the place of the other little girl, for this mother who would later relate how she was abandoned too early by her own mother?

Violette's mother was an adult in abeyance[2] who had not yet left childhood. Psychoanalytic knowledge had merely masked her anxiety even more. The first interview gave her the opportunity to speak of the loneliness in which her own mother had left her, and also of her disagreements with her husband: she had always wanted him to take on the role of a loving mother, but he, of course, could not measure up to that expectation. Didn't the second daughter's name emphasize the mother's disappointment?

This first interview also gave Violette the chance to hear that a drama was being repeated that went beyond her own hatred of Marie. She hadn't even met her little sister yet. She had before her only the image of a frightening enemy, her mother's enemy as well as her own, someone who bore little resemblance to Marie. It was this fantasmatic enemy that she had tried to choke. Understanding this was our task in her therapy.

---

2. Translator's note: Again, *en souffrance* means both "in abeyance" and "in suffering."

9

Lolita, the "Abnormal" Child

She was 11 when we first met, a pretty, blond girl, quite small. Her eyes were sad and she did not smile. She seemed lifeless and resigned. She was accompanied by her parents.

> *Father:* We came to see you because Lolita has always been handicapped. But don't ask how or why, since we don't know. A mistake during the delivery? An illness at the fetal stage? A genetic problem? There are no end of medical charts, but we've never been able to see them.
>
> *C.M.* (to Mother): How were your pregnancy and delivery?
>
> *Mother:* Fine. I felt well when I was pregnant. I didn't expect to have a handicapped child! But I'm convinced that the delivery went well; she was normal when she came out of my belly. But as for what happened afterwards, I can't say, because the doctors were in charge, not me.

Resuscitation had not been necessary at the time of the birth, but Lolita had been hospitalized. She had been a full-term baby, but the obstetrician was concerned about the results of her clinical examination and referred her to the neonatology service. "She's tired," the parents were told, "hardly reactive, hypotonic. More tests are needed." When she was handed over to her parents three weeks later, the prognosis was unfavorable, but the doctors offered no diagnosis. There was no named illness, no causal explanation, just dreadful prophecies for the future: "You have to expect serious problems. We don't know whether she'll ever walk or talk. We can't say exactly what will happen, but one thing is certain, and that's that there'll be consequences and she'll be handicapped."

What consequences? No one knew, and the parents had no new information to add. When I saw her, Lolita could walk, run, and speak, but her gait was uncoordinated, her use of language was usually at the level of echolalia, and her general psychomotor development was retarded. She had recently become able to use the toilet during the day, but her mother still diapered her at night. She avoided contact with other children and was fearful of adults. On occasion she would throw violent tantrums that frightened those around her.

The parents had never wanted any more children, so she was alone at home. Given her handicap, they had no hope of educating her. The mother had given up her career to be Lolita's full-time nurse. Twice a year she was seen at the neurology service of the hospital where she had been cared for as a baby, and the senior physician who was following the case was quite puzzled: "It's incredible," he had told the parents during the most recent visit:

> Your daughter wasn't supposed to walk or talk. She has brain damage; her CT and MRI scans are clear on that. It's really astounding. Her development will certainly stop soon. She'll

get more and more angry and there'll be more crises. You have to institutionalize her, or she'll wear you out in a few years if you're not careful!

But the parents wanted to fight for this little girl, to give her everything. They knew she would be their only child. Besides, the doctor had once said that there might be some genetic problem with the parents in such cases. But what kind of case was it?

While her parents were talking, Lolita played with the puppets. Not missing a word of what was said, she looked at her mother out of the corner of her eye and seemed to watch for my reactions. Her brain damage did not prevent her from being extremely present. She began to play fighting games with the puppets and glided over to her mother, whom she began to attack likewise: "The crocodile is eating you up, he's devouring you. The wolf is devouring you." And to Father: "The wolf is stronger than you"; and again to Mother: "Tremble, tremble, you're going to die."

Now the mother had had enough, and she raised her voice in anger:

> *Mother:* Stop, Lolita. You're wearing me out. I'm trying to talk with the doctor, so stop. Why do you have it in for me? Don't I do everything for you? Why are we here? For you, again!"
>
> *Father:* My wife is really at the end of her rope. We came to ask whether you know what's wrong with Lolita. Apparently there are kinds of illness that psychoanalysts know about and neurologists don't.

What could I say to these parents? How could I understand them? Exhausted by the terrible ordeals they had been through since Lolita's birth, they could speak only of symptoms, diagnoses, of MRI and CT scans. They had no strength left with which to talk about themselves or the child. What did they expect from psychoanalysis? A super-knowledge that could give answers where a professor of neurology couldn't? Or could they be asking an entirely different question about their desire for the life, or the death, of this child?

Lolita remained alive and, despite all the problems she had encountered in putting herself together, fully involved. She began telling her true story right in this first hour. When I turned to her to ask what she thought, she replied, before her dumbfounded parents: "Y' see, the problem is that I scare Mom too much."

Many preliminary sessions with Lolita and her parents were needed before she and I could begin a course of psychotherapy. And much patience was called for before her voice could be given back to this girl who had so much to say. Her parents, who had left everything to medicine, now re-evaluated the way they conceptualized the situation. Little by little, they allowed themselves to talk about their suffering and that of their daughter, and to grant Lolita a role other than that of an object of scientific study. This was a rebirth for her, and, for the parents, a true encounter, one that had not been possible before, with their child.

10

Adrien, the Tiger, and the "Didy"

Adrien had been referred by his pediatrician. He was a lively, rather cheerful 4 year old, but he was always sick: sore throats, ear infections, indigestion, stomach aches. Hardly a week went by that Adrien did not see a doctor. His frequent illnesses kept him out of school, but, his mother explained, this wasn't a problem because he didn't like going there.

C.M.: You don't like school, Adrien?

Adrien got up on his mother's lap and looked at her.

Mother: Come on, Adrien, answer when someone asks you
   a question.
Adrien: Don't know.
Mother: Well, I do. The teacher complains about him a lot.
   He's withdrawn, doesn't move, doesn't participate in
   anything. He comes to school with his didy [the diaper that he had kept with him since infancy] and his

stuffed tiger. He holds the didy in one hand and the tiger in the other and refuses to join in the circle because he's afraid he'll drop his precious treasures. So he sits in a corner and clutches them and sucks his thumb. His father is getting sick because of these two things he never lets go of, but I don't want to traumatize him. I won't take them away by force; he's got enough problems as it is.

C.M.: What problems?

Mother: Well, he's sick so much, and at 8 months he was hospitalized for ten days with a bad case of laryngitis. They took him away from me by force. He was screaming, I was crying—it was horrible. Since then, he's always been sick. My husband has no idea what's going on, and I'm wearing myself out taking care of Adrien all the time and protecting him from my husband. Some days I ask myself if I should get a divorce, so I could be alone with him and take better care of him.

I also learned that Adrien still had a bottle in the morning and used a diaper at night. I noticed that he was looking at the felt-tip pens on my desk. When I asked him whether he'd like to draw, he took them and gave them to Mother so she could draw for him.

C.M.: Adrien, I'm suggesting that *you* draw. You don't have to if you don't want to, but it seemed as though you'd like to. With your own head and your own hands you can make a picture.

For the rest of the hour Adrien drew broken objects, figures without arms or hands, and cars that didn't go.

The early separation about which his mother spoke at length seems to have left both of them injured. They had been apart, without words to help them symbolize the absence and thus endure it better—just the Real of these two bodies that were like one body torn in half. Both Adrien and his mother had remained ill afterwards, and in order to protect him she wanted to separate him once again, but this time from his father. She feared any intervention of the law.

Adrien's development had been arrested. He could not be aggressive or get into conflict with his excessively fragile mother or with the father who was kept from him. Nor could he encounter other children in school: burdened with the tiger and the didy, he couldn't even hold out his hand to them. He withdrew within himself and could only absent himself from all human contact. He didn't know high from low, left from right. Why should he, since Mother held the compass? Neither his broken body nor his genital belonged to him: "It's Mommy," he said, "who knows if I make peepee in bed or not."

If Adrien could speak, express his death wishes and his aggressivity, all these illnesses would disappear. But was Mother ready for such a change?

> *Mother:* The pediatrician said we should see a psychoanalyst, just two or three times, because it's not good for him to be so shy. But do you think he's shy? I also wanted to ask you whether homeopathy might help him, so that he wouldn't catch cold so often. The pediatrician said you'd be able to answer all these questions. Nowadays, it's psychoanalysts who have all the answers for moms, isn't it?

Well, one thing is certain, and that's that psychoanalysts have to deal with all those questions. Parents' questions, doctors' questions, and the questions they ask themselves. Sometimes the nature of the pediatrician's referral determines a certain type of consultation, and analysts stay within these limits. Is it always possible to go further? To ask questions in a different way? Françoise Dolto once said, in a seminar: "Sometimes, when parents come for a consultation, they're willing to climb only 300 meters, and you're not going to be able to get them to climb Mont Blanc."

It all depends on their fragility, the degree of their suffering. But it is also the case that, after an initial visit, many parents undertake real analytic work. One can't generalize. If it is true that the mode of referral can preclude work with a child and stop communication, it is also true that it can open up the possibility of analysis.

How do those who most often refer to us, namely pediatricians, speak of psychoanalysis to families?

11

From the Pediatrician
to the Psychoanalyst: "Fix this Child"

A pediatrician can make a referral to a psychoanalyst in several ways, and these various styles leave their imprint on the initial interview and form the basis of our work. Of course, there are still many pediatricians who do not send on their patients, either for fear of losing them ("Since the time when I referred this family to you, they have not returned") or because they see no purpose in it, believing that they themselves can hear what the patients have to say. Are they afraid of charlatanism? They can't always be blamed for that. Some of them conceal their fear of analysis by claiming that they do not see it as being serious, scientific. In this way they often rationalize their difficulty in facing their own unconscious and what it is trying to say.

Among the pediatricians who do refer patients to us there is a wide variety of approaches. At the two extremes—which sometimes meet—we find the conscientious ones, those who give the parents our name after they have tried everything. The only thing left is psychotherapy. Why not? At least no one will be able to say they didn't think of it. In the belief (which shows how little faith they have in analysis) that, if it doesn't help, at least it can't hurt, they send us their patients with a clear conscience, which is not the same thing as a clear unconscious. Pediatricians are not machines for handing out prescriptions, but subjects, and as such are caught up in the discourse of the unconscious. When a pediatrician makes a referral, this has consequences for him and for his patient.

It isn't surprising that the parents sent by these conscientious doctors come with a demand that is the mirror image of the pediatrician's: "At least no one can say we didn't try everything; I don't want to have to reproach myself later on." For these pediatricians, analysis is usually just a kind of extra remediation. One more or less believes in it, and it's part of the therapeutic repertoire, so the child might as well be "referred" in order to be "reformed."

A prescription for thirty sessions: "Dear Colleague, I am referring Philippe to you in connection with problems of a psycho-somatic nature." This hyphen linking psyche and soma actually marks their radical separation. Every kind of test was performed on the child, and nothing turned up. But the physician, having rather naively thought that, in ordering many tests to be done, he would be reassuring the parents and the child, doesn't understand why they are more anxious than ever when the tests come back negative.

As Lacan said, hysteria needs to be identified, not to be cured. In such cases the child we see for the first time is often a depressed one. Medicine does not take him seriously and wants nothing more to do with him, because it has found nothing. The issue of diagnosis is complex, and most often the pediatrician refrains from any explanation to the family on the grounds that there is no diagnosis: "It's probably just nerves." Freud, however, made it clear that analytic treatment cannot be indicated by default, that it must be undertaken only under specific conditions. He (1900) discusses this eloquently in connection with a patient whose symptoms suggested a serious organic problem:

> It would have been tempting to diagnose a neurosis (which would have solved every difficulty), if only the patient had not repudiated with so much energy the sexual history without which I refuse to recognize the presence of a neurosis. In my embarrassment I sought help from the physician whom I, like many other people, respect more than any as a man and before whose authority I am readiest to bow. He listened to my doubts, told me they were justified, and then gave his opinion: "Keep the man under observation; it must be a neurosis." Since I knew he did not share my views on the etiology of the neuroses, I did not produce any counter-argument, but I made no concealment of my scepticism. A few days later I informed the patient that I could do nothing for him and recommended him to seek other advice. Whereupon, to my intense astonishment, he started apologizing for having lied to me. He had been much too ashamed of himself, he said, and went on to reveal precisely the piece of sexual etiology which I had been expecting and without which I had been unable to accept his illness as a neurosis. I was relieved but at the same time humiliated. I had to admit that my consultant . . . had seen more clearly than I had. [pp. 300–301]

Note how strongly Freud insists that a diagnosis cannot be made in the absence of signs. For him, there is no question of sending a patient for analysis just because no other cause has been found. And let us also note that he consults a physician (one who, it seems, had different opinions) in order to ask advice. This external advice serves to send him back to work and perhaps enables him to listen to his patient in a different way.

The professional collaboration is therefore neither embarrassing nor useless.

In contrast to the conscientious pediatricians I have just mentioned, there is another type of doctor, the "mystic," for whom there is no salvation without analysis. He has the idea that "it's all in the head," that he would see few patients were it not for anxiety on the part of the parents. In these cases there is no physical examination. The physician removes his stethoscope and does not weigh or measure the child but instead asks him to draw his family. He sees him regularly for some time before referring him to us when symptoms persist: "We need to call in a specialist." He gives the family our address as if it were the date and the time for the next train to Lourdes.

12

Listening to Carla's Heart

A 9-year-old girl who had been referred by one of the "mystical" pediatricians complained about her heart:

> Please, please listen to my heart. The doctor said there's no point listening to it; he said the trouble's in my head. But my head doesn't hurt. I'm afraid all the time that my heart's going to burst. So I'll do what the doctor said and talk to you, but first I want to know how my heart is.

It took me a long time to persuade the pediatrician to agree to see her again and examine her, since he was sure an examination was not called for. No doubt he was right: no examination was not called for, but a medical gesture was. This gesture was necessary for Carla to be able to formulate a demand and to begin work on her own behalf.

Many months passed before she could let her heart and her suffering be heard in a way that the stethoscope could not manage. If the doctor refuses to take into account the initial "demand for medical attention," he can prevent the child from seeing an analyst. Likewise, if the analyst refuses to hear a question asked of the doctor, even if it appears transferentially, the child may not be able to take advantage of analysis. For it is not only among physicians that we encounter resistances. Some analysts, blinded by a need for power, think they have all the answers and scorn medical knowledge on the grounds that it is mechanical. Can there be any defense for these one-man-bands who know all and can cure all ills? Are we supposed to think that it would be fatal not to have completed an analysis?

What kind of odd belief system would we then find ourselves in? Are we in the middle of a fairy tale, in which we are magicians who are consulted in order to exorcise the prophecies of doctors? Do we really believe ourselves capable of performing miracle cures? If taken to its extreme, this perversion of the idea of abstinence would lead to the dream of a faultless analyst who no longer had any desire. A sphinx identified with his own silence, he would be able to do everything and feel nothing.

Avoiding the traps of the imaginary* does not mean forgetting the analyst's desire:

_____

* Lacanian psychoanalysis reads Freud in a way that breaks down the classical dichotomies between nature and culture, individual and society, and inner and outer reality. The real, the imaginary, and the symbolic decompose the psyche into three categories instead of two. The real is reality in its unmediated form. It is what disrupts the subject's received notions about himself and the world around him. Thus it characteristically appears to the subject as a shattering enigma, because in order to make sense of it he or she will have to symbolize it, that is, to find signifiers that can ensure its control. The imaginary is the realm of subjective experience *per se*, the world as it appears to the subject. Lacan explains the genesis of the imaginary in the Mirror Stage, the archaic experience in which the child encounters his or her reflection in the gaze of the (m)Other. From that moment on, both the child's perception of the world and his fantasies will be informed by the experience of such a gaze.

If the analyst embodies the popular image, and also the deontological image, of apathy, it is in so far as he is possessed by a desire stronger than the desires that might be expected, namely to get to the point with his patient, to take him in his arms, or to throw him out the window. . . . The analyst says: I am possessed by a stronger desire. He is justified in saying this as an analyst, inasmuch as there has been a change in the economy of his desire. [Lacan 1960–1961, pp. 220–221]

The analyst's desire is an informed one that enables him to remain alive in order for analysis to take place. He does not have to protect himself against feelings that arise in him within the transference. But if analysis is to be possible, the analysand, too, must remain alive.

On what grounds would an analyst refrain from telling a patient who is complaining of somatic problems to see a doctor? Isn't it rather the case that, by locating the demand elsewhere, by placing the responsibility in an entirely different domain, we can sometimes open up a space in our sessions for the body, in its suffering and its pleasure, as the bearer of truth? As Lacan said, "It is in the register of the manner of response to the patient's demand that the properly medical position has a chance to survive" (1966, p. 20).

We are all aware of the risk of accepting into analysis children with behavioral problems that turn out to be due to brain

---

The symbolic order is the order of language and culture. It is a constraining structure imposed on the child through the Law of the Name of the Father. The repression that this law entails causes the formation of the unconscious. The real, the imaginary, and the symbolic together weave the subject's reality at all times. These categories are always intertwined and are never processed by the subject in their pure or isolated form. Only a psychotic outbreak can undo the knotting of the triad. [JFG]

tumors, diseases of the immune system, or enzyme disorders that are difficult to diagnose. I recall an 8-year-old girl, labeled pseudo-retarded and accordingly seen in psychotherapy, who was belatedly diagnosed with a severe thyroid malfunction. In renouncing omnipotence and risking the abandonment of his so-called technically rigorous position, the analyst can allow himself to listen for the real of a subject's body.

If the pediatrician who refers the child to us entertains the quasi-magical belief that nothing outside of interpretation has any importance, then, I repeat, certain modes of assuming analytic responsibility can be precluded. The parents of a little boy once told me, "Doctor X told us that only you can save our son." For this pediatrician, the time of miracles had come. To be set aright or to be miraculously cured, the child knocks on our door because of the demand of his physician, a demand that cannot be neglected.

Moreover, we almost always find a mirror effect between the way in which the doctor discusses analysis with the family and the style of the first interview with us. The analyst then has to deal with the child's demand (in the best of cases), and also with the demands of the family and the pediatrician, and hence with the consequences of that pediatrician's transference to analysis or, even worse, to the analyst himself. This presents an additional difficulty in working with children: the transference that will be established will at first be directly connected to the pediatrician, who, for the child (and for the parents, who always identify more or less with their child's doctor), is the one who knows what is good for him and is thus the good parent. Hippocrates spoke of the need for the doctor to present a healthy appearance that patients could identify with; Molière, in order to cure the imaginary invalid, suggests that he become a doctor himself, which, as it happened, worked for the patient but not for the author. The imaginary is not so easily detached from the real.

Certain analysts, out of a need to protect themselves, choose abstinence and sever all ties with the doctor. Others, despite the difficulties it entails, try to work with him. Sometimes the medical aspect is so salient for a child that it is hard not to take it into account. This was the case with Anna, a girl of 14.

13

Anna

A year earlier, she had become interested in attracting boys and to this end decided that she had to go on a diet. She lost weight so rapidly that she weighed only eighty-six pounds when the school doctor called her parents in. They had noticed the weight loss, but had said nothing: Anna was free to do as she wished with her body. The school doctor then referred her to me. She came alone. Her parents, unwilling to accompany her, had said, "It's your concern. You're a free agent, old enough to be in charge of your life."

Anna was terrified. She told me about feeling that her body was being transformed at night, her legs getting thinner, her arms changing shape. The other morning she had stood in front of the mirror and not seen herself, as if the mirror were empty of her image. For five or six years eyes had been following her wherever she went. She was sure that they were there to judge her. Once she had begun to diet, she knew she would not be able to stop; she was heading for death and could do nothing about it.

As she spoke in the sessions, she was afraid that she would empty herself out with all these words. Fortunately, she knew that I would interrupt at the end of the hour, and this break made it possible for her to talk. She no longer trusted herself. The scale that she checked each morning couldn't be trusted either, since, she thought, it was looking at her with its eyes. Our sessions were full of tears, anguish, and pleas: "Don't let me die," even if this prayer, in the transference, was addressed to others.

I suggested she return to the school doctor and ask her to take over the case: to see Anna once a week and weigh her, treat her medically, and take care of her. Anna was begging for protection of this body that was getting away from her at the very moment when sexuality became an issue. It was too early to interpret the transference, too early even to talk about her parents.

As medical treatment put her somewhat out of danger, Anna became able to work in the sessions on the object of her desire, on her fantasy. Her weight stabilized, and there was no longer a need to consider hospitalization. The parents finally came, at their daughter's request. Far from being a kind of supplementary insurance, the medical monitoring made it possible for Anna to use psychotherapy. The doctor's detailed answers to the girl's questions, her wish to keep her alive—that is, to do her job as a doctor—enabled Anna to tolerate the analytic situation.

This doctor never played analyst and never treated Anna's questions as absurd from a medical point of view. The desire to know is the first manifestation of sexual life; it is what the patient demands. The doctor answered in a way that allowed Anna to formulate these questions differently. She never thought that her patient's problems were just a matter of pounds to be lost or gained. She knew her role and helped Anna to get out of the impasse in which she had been trapped. That kind of knowledge is not learned from books.

14

Alexandre, or the Broken Piano

Alexandre was a boy of ten, physically disabled as a result of brain damage caused by a brief respiratory failure during birth. He spoke poorly and could talk only with much difficulty. He was a brilliant student, but his body could not follow suit. He was like a virtuoso whose only available instrument is a broken piano.

The previous year Alexandre had had his annual appointment with the chief of the neurology service. Afterwards he had shut himself up in his room and refused to go to school. He asked everyone to leave him alone. He didn't care! He preferred the wheelchair to the pressure put on him by the orthopedists.

He was oppositional and depressed when I saw him at our first appointment. All he could talk about was the injustice, the powerlessness, the weariness of the situation in which he was immersed. Caught between revolt and despair, he had no more strength left with which to struggle.

He spoke of the consultation with the neurologist. "I'm fed up with doctors," he said.

I asked what he had been told. "Nothing," he replied. "I tried to see his eyes, but it was hard, because he wasn't looking at me."

"Maybe he was talking to your parents?"

"No, my mom said he was adding some papers to my chart."

Every year Alexandre was brought before a specialist who didn't look at him. I therefore suggested to his parents to take him to a pediatrician whom I respected. He was seen four times a year by this doctor, in addition to the annual appointment with the neurologist, which Alexandre learned to put in perspective. Alexandre told me that the pediatrician saw him alone, graphed his progress in a large notebook, explained all his interventions, and encouraged him to keep track of his development and growth. The notebook belonged to Alexandre: he was to keep it with him, as it was his, and bring it to each appointment. This did not resolve Alexandre's problems, but he was able to speak of his unhappiness and anxiety.

Another pediatrician might have seen no point in the notebook, but this one knew how important it was for the child. And it was certainly just as comforting for Alexandre to know that, while I recognized his physical suffering, in contrast to the others in his environment I did not pretend to be able to rehabilitate him.

For Alexandre, going to this pediatrician meant that his body now belonged to him, just like the precious notebook. He spoke of both the pediatrician and the notebook in our sessions, and, with the doctor, sometimes talked about his analysis. He knew that both of us, analyst and physician, were committed to the same project of offering him different spaces in which he could, if he chose, "manage" his illness and examine his desire. He knew that we were acquainted with one another and might occasionally discuss him without—as he knew from experience—any violation of the confidentiality of the analytic sessions.

This connection was as important for him as a safety net is for a trapeze artist: the doctor and I were the guarantors of a space in which he could risk envisioning a life for himself. For certain children with physical ailments, collaboration between their doctor and their analyst is essential, provided that the roles are clearly defined and not interchangeable, and that the confidentiality of the sessions and respect for the child are always in the foreground.

It is in this context of acceptance of radically different roles, and of respect for the child and his family, that a physician's referral to an analyst becomes possible. Turning one's back on medicine is untherapeutic: "It is in treating the somatic illness, while at the same time remaining psychoanalytically receptive to what is wrong *elsewhere*, that the doctor helps the mother herself to make the displacement that she has refused to make" (Mannoni 1964, pp. 15–16). This stepping aside with regard to the initial demand is what the physician can enable the family to do. When, as a result, the question can be reformulated, then the psychoanalyst is able to come in and take charge. Without this preliminary approach, analytic work is more often than not doomed to failure, with the analyst becoming a "super-pediatrician" who is supposed to "cure" the patient on whom medicine has given up.

Part II

From the
First Session to
the Analytic Treatment

15

Xénophon, or the Name-Crosses[1]

Xénophon was 4 when we first met. A small, scrawny child, he seemed fragile and timid. Keeping his gaze averted, he was silent and did not answer when spoken to. The teacher at the kindergarten he had been attending since the beginning of the year had called his behavior to the attention of the school doctor.

In class he did not play with the other children but sat motionless in a corner without even looking at them, constantly jerking his hands about in front of his eyes or looking at the ceiling, lost in mute contemplation. If an adult tried to engage him or get him to participate in an activity, he would become panicky and begin to scream.

The school doctor referred him to a general practitioner, who confirmed the diagnosis of autism and referred him to a

---

1. As a consultant for a hospital, I saw Xénophon from the beginning to the end of his treatment. It is rare that analytic work can be done in these circumstances, and I want to thank the senior physician, Dr. Abram Coen, who made it possible for me to take on this case.

child psychiatry service, where I saw him in order to, as his mother put it, discuss institutionalizing him. Accompanying him to the first interview, she seemed surprised by how concerned the doctors and the school were. "Of course," she said, "he's a bit babyish, a bit slow, and it's true that his three big sisters overprotect him and play with him as if he were a doll, spoiling him and dressing him up as a girl. But he's so gentle, so sensitive—it can't hurt him to be spoiled a little."

At home he didn't speak and was able to pronounce only a few isolated, barely understandable words. And he refused to eat, became enraged for no apparent reason, and had great difficulty falling asleep. He was encopretic and enuretic. "I'm sure that'll pass once he's grown up," Mother said. For the time being, she concluded, all he had to do was make up his mind to grow up.

At the end of this initial session I asked Xénophon whether he wanted to stay alone with me. Without giving him a chance to indicate anything, his mother thrust him from her arms, in which he had been curled up, put him on the chair, and left the room without a word. Xénophon did not cry. He just sat there as if he were not even present. I noticed at once that he avoided my gaze, which seemed to me *a priori* to contradict the diagnosis of autism made by the doctors who had seen him. If I spoke to him, he became panic-stricken, began to cry, and rushed toward the door. As soon as I stopped speaking, he calmed down and became mute and inexpressive.

I then tried to put words to his fear. I established a frame and told him that we weren't at home or in school, that I wasn't going to ask him anything, that he could take the crayons, the paper, and the clay that were there on the desk for him, but he didn't have to do or say anything. He immediately quieted down, and, taking the ashtray from my desk and spinning it like a top, became entranced by the sight and the metallic sound of this object. Against this noisy background there was silence. And that is how things might well have remained, had I not noticed some notes I had taken while Mother was talking. It occurred to me to read them aloud, as if in a voice-over telling a story, without speaking directly to him: "Xénophon is a little boy of 4, born after three sisters. At school he always seems to be afraid. At home he has trouble sleeping and sometimes gets very angry. His mommy says that he is like a doll for his sisters." Xénophon dropped his improvised top and began listening closely to me. Still not speaking directly to him, I asked: "What could this little boy be so afraid of? Does he want somebody to help him? Would he come back to see me again?"

Very solemnly, Xénophon got up from the chair, took from my hand the felt-tip pen with which I had written the notes, and, as if it were a signature, made a St. Andrew's cross at the bottom of the page. For a split second our eyes met, and I understood that, in this fleeting moment, he was completely present. It was with this sign, the meaning of which I would come to understand much later, that his analysis got underway.

In the following sessions I initially saw him with his mother and then alone. When he was alone he was often extremely anxious, and he tended to withdraw and isolate himself. I respected this symptom; there was no need to combat it in the sessions but rather to try to let "it," the unconscious, speak of the symptom. I gradually learned from the mother how afraid the parents were of losing him. Refusing to leave him, they never went out lest something happen to him in their absence. They did not leave him in anyone's care and had him sleep in their room so that nothing would happen to him during the night.

The mother spoke, in Xénophon's presence, of her own history. The third in a family of six children, she took care of all the siblings like a mother. Her oldest brother was handicapped and was unable to do anything around the house. The doctor said his brain didn't work normally and got him a disability card. He now lived in an institution and was considered to have a mental age of about 12. After the birth of Xénophon's mother came two girls and a boy; the youngest child was also handicapped. In speaking of him the mother pointed out a resemblance between him and Xénophon: he too had not wanted to grow up and had dropped out of school.

She spoke of her own mother as being always ill and tired, and as often saying that she should never have had children. The parents fought often. She feared her strict father although, fleeing a home that he described as bleak and wearing, he was away most of the time. The oldest girl, she had taken care of everything and recalled having been very sad about not being able to help her mother with the illness that kept her bedridden, an illness that the doctors were unable to explain or to name. (In the nineteenth century it would no doubt have been called languor or consumption.) As she recounted her story, she asked: "Do you think this means anything for Xénophon? How can he understand all this?"

Xénophon was careful to be withdrawn in her presence and did not show himself until later, when we were alone and I re-read my notes as I had done during the first session. He had kept the habit of marking the end of each session with a sign, a sign that became a drawing. He was now beginning to draw and would take a sheet of paper for himself instead of making a mark on mine. His first drawings were crosses (Figure 1) and sketches of people, most often overlapping (Figure 2), then represented by two before they could tolerate becoming "one" (Figure 3).

During this time he was still silent, but he became more willing to communicate with me, looking at me a bit more and answering with a gesture of his head when I asked him some-

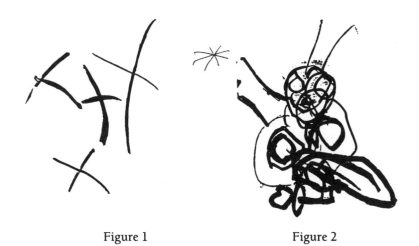

Figure 1   Figure 2

Figure 3

thing. In the eighth session the mother spoke of the dramatic death of her younger sister. She wept bitterly and said she had never gotten over the loss of this baby, whom she had brought up as her own. "She was my very own doll," she said. The sister had died of a brain tumor at the age of two and a half. Xénophon's mother had been 13 at the time. She thought that her older brother, the handicapped one, in his wish to be like her and take care of the baby, had dropped the child. Enormous guilt had made mourning for the little sister even more impossible. The mother said that she too had wanted to die on the day of the funeral and that she had often thought of death when Xénophon, her much-wished-for boy, was a baby. Moreover, the birth of the last of the mother's siblings, a much-desired boy after three girls, occurred on the day her sister died.

After this session Xénophon drew a figure and barred its mouth with a grate (Figure 4).

I asked: "He can't talk?" Xénophon replied by placing a finger in front of his mouth as if indicating that silence must be respected.

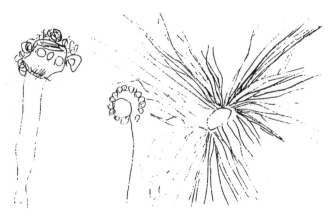

Figure 4

Although I had asked to see him right from the outset, the father did not come until the tenth session. He had always put off an appointment because of one obstacle or another. And indeed there were obstacles for this father. Obstacles to his working, since he was unemployed, to his speaking, since he would become tongue-tied in fear, obstacles to his being a father to Xénophon, whom he resented. "Three children are enough," he said. And Xénophon was so attached to his mother that the father could not talk with him or take care of him. In any case, he said, Xénophon did not want him: "It's easy to see that he doesn't like me." In another session the mother said of this anxious and depressed man: "It's like having another child at home. I'm the one who makes all the decisions; I keep track of our finances and give him pocket money. When he's not feeling well, he drinks. He never says anything. He'd be lost without me."

Xénophon's father had been the third of four boys in his family of origin. He described his mother as a strong woman who was in charge of the household. His father, a timid and retiring man, had died when Xénophon's father was 15. "That's the time when I needed him most. Before that, I didn't have time to talk to him, or maybe I didn't have the courage."

Xénophon's father, despite the phobic symptoms that made life difficult for him, came regularly to the sessions and made a lot of progress at the same time as his son did. He spoke, among other things, of his great distress at the birth of his younger brother, who, he feared, would usurp his place with the mother. Xénophon's birth had rekindled his anxiety. He had not wanted a boy—especially a much-resented fourth child—who might once again take his place, and once again he felt terribly guilty.

It was only after the first conjoint sessions with the father that Xénophon began to speak, or rather to whisper, forming words without raising his voice. At this time he drew a man, again with a grill over his mouth. (See Figure 5). "He knows," Xénophon said, "but he doesn't speak." These were the first words he had said in our sessions.

In the next hour he drew crosses similar to those he had drawn at the bottom of my sheet of paper on the first day. But this time he whispered, "These are name-crosses. To make a name, you have to have a cross." (See Figure 6).

I noticed that this cross resembled the X of Xénophon. I told him this, and he replied with what must surely be called his poem. He repeated: "Yes, the name-crosses." I asked: "Whose names?" "The names of the dead. Shh—mustn't talk." "Why?"

Because I don't have a peenie.
I have a thingie because I'm afraid.
Noise makes me afraid.
The name-crosses make fears come.
They make tears come.

In the next hour Mother explained that she often visited the grave, marked with a cross, of Xénophon's little sister. She

Figure 5

Figure 6

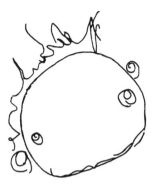

Figure 7

took him along, laid flowers on the grave, and sometimes wept. For several months after this session Xénophon drew himself as a little girl with no mouth (Figure 7).

I spoke to him about his mother's grief for the baby, and of the flowers placed on the grave. He called them tears. For several sessions he drew "mommy's tears" (Figure 8).

Very gradually, he began to live in his little boy's body. It was at this time that he happened to discover a baby bottle in the toy box; he immediately filled it and drank from it with great

Figure 8

pleasure. The next ten sessions began with his savoring the bottle. I neither forbade nor encouraged this but spoke of the time when, as a baby, he had had such trouble with his bottles. Now he drew figures whom he named "little boy" (Figures 9 and 10).

Houses appeared. At this time his father began to take an interest in him. In one session that was of great significance for Xénophon's development, the father said: "I'm now beginning to realize that I have a son." Xénophon thereupon drew little boys and said: "He's little. His daddy wants him to grow up, but mommy wants a baby in her stomach. Mustn't be afraid." At the same time, he began to show interest in reading and writing. Now allowed to attend school, he was in first grade and was getting speech therapy.

When putting his crosses on paper, he was able to make a distinction between a line that happens to look like a letter and

Figure 9

Figure 10

a letter that is part of a signifier. But nothing put a halt to the endless sliding of signifiers* that began with the cross of his name, and Xénophon was bewildered. When it came to his

---

*Lacan reinterpreted Saussure's distinctions between language/speech and signifier/signified in order to show how the structure of the unconscious and the structure of language have similar modes of operation. For Saussure, speech is determined by a system of values (language) that operates beyond the individual's control. The relation between a concept and its acoustic image does not result from a particular affinity between a word and its referent but is determined by the other signs that compose a given language. In that sense, the arbitrary relation between signifier and signified shows that language is an entity with its own laws and regulations that operate independently of the realm of existence that it represents. For Lacan, the dividing line between the signifier and the signified expresses the problematic relation between what is said consciously and what is barred from conscious discourse: "[W]e can say that it is in the chain of the signifiers that the meaning 'insists' but that none of its elements 'consists' in the signification of which it is at the moment capable. We are forced, then, to accept the notion of an incessant sliding of the signified under the signifier" (1977, pp. 153-154). [JFG]

mother's desire, there was a void of which she was unable to speak, and the child was in danger of being swallowed up by this void, this terrifying hole. Xénophon's drawings now always included a house with a little girl shut up inside, motionless. Near the house there was a little boy, but outside, as if free, detached from her (Figure 11). From the time he started this new series of drawings, he stopped drinking from the bottle in our sessions.

It is clear that a child's drawing is to be interpreted the same way as the discourse of an adult, but—as is also the case with adults—always in an interrogative mode, as if suggesting a working hypothesis while remaining open to being questioned and surprised. It is always the child who instructs. As Freud said, we have to be wary of presuppositions and prejudices. The only thing we have to go on in the sessions, and especially when we make interpretations, is what the patient, adult or child, has brought in. It is important to avoid being drawn into interpretative frenzies concerning these drawings, and, with drawings as with dreams, to stay close to the patient's associations.

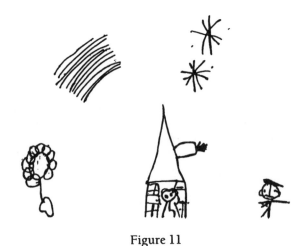

Figure 11

As the analysis progressed, Xénophon progressed along with it and became able to articulate his fears. It took six years of analysis before he could begin to let go of his paralyzing anxiety. The emergence of phobias enabled him to fear specific things that could be named: he was afraid of being devoured and he was also afraid of small animals, because, he said, "they make love." He drew them (Figure 12).

He was also afraid of the air he breathed, of pictures he looked at, of noises he heard, of all forms of violence, of meat (which he refused to eat), and above all else of the elevator.[2] He made a drawing of himself in the midst of fears (Figure 13).

It is understandable how a child with this many phobic symptoms could cut himself off from the world and withdraw into an autistic defensive system that was, however, neither true autism

Figure 12

2. Translator's note: *L'ascenseur* ("the elevator") is homonymous with *la "sans soeur"* ("the 'without a sister'").

Figure 13

nor psychosis. Labeled autistic before his analysis, Xénophon could now speak and was beginning to read and write. No institutionalization was required. How many children have their lives destroyed by this type of diagnosis, just because they were once unable to meet the gaze of a psychiatrist, a doctor, or a psychologist? A life can hang in the balance of a gaze.

Xénophon needed speech therapy in order to be able to stay in school and gradually to master his fear of reading and writing. But was it writing he feared, or the appearance of a sign that would be more than a sign, one that would be on the way to becoming a signifier? Surely that was what was at the root of his fear.

Simultaneously, in different registers, the analysis enabled him to find out that it was the signifier of his name that had made it impossible for him to write, to separate from the little girl and mourn her, and to turn toward his father, who, for his part, had progressed to the point where he could be approached by his son and finally acknowledge him.

In the final months of Xénophon's analysis, his mother often complained about him: he was becoming tough, did not obey her, no longer let his sisters dress him up. She felt sad and depressed without being able to say why, and was surprised that Xénophon had suddenly taken a strong interest in tinkering about with his father; he wanted to imitate the father, stole his razor and cologne, and tried on his neckties. She made a suicide attempt, a desperate cry for help at a time when her son was beginning to live his own life in a boy's body, and to risk speech. At this time Xénophon drew a building without a roof, a building, he explained, that had an elevator. No one wanted to live in that building anymore. The man in the picture was protected by a cloud of stars. These stars were actually the crosses from the early sessions, but now they were tamed, he seemed to be saying, and useful: "Those crosses are star crosses and you need them to live; it's not like crosses for dead people." (See Figure 14.)

Figure 14

It is likely that Xénophon knew how to speak before he began analysis; a child doesn't just begin to talk all at once, as he did. He could talk but didn't, like the man in his drawings with the grill over his mouth. He was mute. For his mother, the little dead sister was mute forever. The mother said so herself in one of the sessions: this baby was like her doll. Freud notes that little girls use dolls to replace the missing penis; hadn't the loss of her little sister reconfirmed the loss of her penis for the mother? At 13, when she had already started menstruating, she lost a baby just when she was becoming able to have one. Later on she wanted a son, but without having mourned the sister who was her imaginary phallus.* As we know, a child always identifies with what concerns the mother most. Xénophon had identified with the object in the tomb. Thus there was no need for him to talk: he was as silent as the grave. The frequent visits to the cemetery, his mother's tears, had made the cross into a phallic object, symbolized and inscribed in stone.

The living Xénophon had replaced this object, filling the mother's void. If his story reveals certain schematic elements of Lacan's theory of the father/mother/child triangle and then of the mother/child/phallus triangle, this history is nonetheless complicated by the oedipal history of the father, who had lost his own father at age 15 and whose mother had found consolation only in her youngest son. And, as for the mother's history, why did the death of the little sister have such a catastrophic

---

*In Lacanian theory, the phallus is the organizing principle of the dynamic of the subject's desire. Whereas, in the individual's fantasy world, the phallus acts as an imaginary object that the subject will first want to incarnate and then move on to have (or seek in a romantic partner) within the symbolic order— that is, in the unconscious realm—the phallus operates as the signifier of a loss, the symbol of the lack of complementarity between the sexes. [JFG]

effect? At what phase of the mother's own oedipal development did this bereavement occur? What role did her little handicapped brother, the only boy in the family, play for her?

A baby is usually given to understand right from his earliest exchanges with his mother that she does not "all" belong to him. She always has interests elsewhere and is drawn to other things; she comes and goes. It is in this play of presence and absence, this lack in which the phallus will assume its place, that the child constructs himself, imagines, symbolizes.* Mother is not all his, and he is not her all. In the defile of the Oedipus, as Lacan calls it, the child encounters the father, renounces the fantasy of being his mother's ideal, accepts castration, and inherits an ego ideal. It is then that the father has played his role: there is no *Verwerfung* (foreclosure), and the child is not psychotic. The Name of the Father has made a quilting point (*point de capiton*), arresting the slide of meanings. Only when the child

---

*The concept of lack, *manque à être*, refers to Lacan's theory of symbolic castration. For Freud, the resolution of the Oedipus complex is dependent on the boy's fear of castration and the girl's penis envy, whereas for Lacan both sexes must undergo the same painful but necessary process that symbolic castration entails. Lacan links the child's submission to the prohibition of incest to his or her entrance into the structure of language. The human being's capacity to symbolize is dependent on his or her acceptance of a loss, the loss of an imaginary complementarity with the mother. As Hegel pointed out, the word is the murder of the thing. This loss consists in giving up one's privileged position as the mother's phallus in order to position oneself in the social world as someone who "has the phallus" or "does not have it." Meeting this almost impossible challenge, which Lacan calls symbolic castration, will offer the individual the bittersweet guarantee that his or her desire will never die off, because it will always remain dependent on the desire of the other. The hope of finding the phallus—in the imaginary—that will guarantee the complementarity between the sexes will always be postponed, since the phallic signifier, as it is operative in the unconscious, causes desire precisely because it is the signifier of lack. [JFG]

is no longer subjected to his mother's desire can he emerge as a subject in his own right. This "desubjection" occurs by way of the law of the father.

Little Hans (Freud 1909) was phobic. Because he was unable to free himself of the phobia, we must conclude that, for him, "the paternal metaphor was not fully operative. For it to take effect, the signifier of the Name of the Father must come to occupy the place in which the child had encountered the desire of the mother" (Faladé 1987, p. 44). Hans's father did not lay down the law to the boy's mother. Hans knew quite well that his mother's desire was elsewhere. To protect himself, he "instituted the horse phobia so that horses could scare him and impose their law" (ibid.). He thereby made a "father" for himself.

Phobia is not neurosis. Like Hans, Xénophon found it very hard to free himself from his mother's desire, to "desubject" himself. And yet he had a father, albeit a weak one. Phobia is, as it were, the garment of neurosis, surrounding and containing it. Hans asked the question of his father, and the father asked Freud the very same question: What is a father? It was the same with Xénophon's father, whose childhood had left him damaged, without guidelines, without an adequate masculine identification.[3] The father is the one who "gives," if only the child is willing to renounce his mother. He gives not only the "no," the prohibition, but also his name,[4] transmitted through his wife, to be the patronymic signifier for the child. And, beyond the name, he gives the child the possibility of being a man in turn. But, like his son, Xénophon's father had problems in this regard.

Colette Misrahi and Serge Hajlblum (1977) make a related point in connection with Little Hans:

---

3. See Dor 1989.
4. Translator's note: Non ("no") and nom ("name") are homonyms.

In the father's answer to Freud, we have to discern an appeal from the father to his son: to introduce him in his own right. If pressure was brought to bear, this was because symbolically Hans was not his child, but rather the child of the transference between Freud and the mother, Freud's former patient, and the father's problem was to enter, at whatever cost, a preformed circuit from which he was excluded. [p. 63]

Let us try to see what it was, in Xénophon's analysis, that changed enough so that the bonds in which he was held prisoner could become somewhat looser. The separation of the cross that was the first letter of his name from the stone cross in the graveyard, and also the fact of his father's word, allowed Xénophon to situate himself differently. Then—and this was essential—his father, acknowledging Xénophon as his son, gave meaning to the desire of the mother. His phrase, "Now I know that I have a son" is without a doubt part of the symbolic and at last enabled Xénophon to be more clearly inscribed in the order of the Name of the Father.

However, although the paternal metaphor had not truly been in effect, we cannot say that this was a case of psychosis, for there was no foreclosure of the Name of the Father. The father had his place in the family; as Mother had said, he was an additional child, and as such he counted for Xénophon. Yet he did not lay down the law for the mother, and, as with Little Hans, his word was not recognized. What Xénophon put in the place of a father was not a horse but a multitude of phobic objects that, because almost everything became forbidden to him, made him increasingly vulnerable to the demands of his superego. Hans was phobic well before his crises, before horses made him so anxious that he was unable to leave the house. Xénophon, as his mutism and his barred mouth indicate, was phobic long before he developed actual phobic objects. The establishment of these objects indicated the dawning of symbolization.

Xénophon's alienation from himself antedated his birth. He arrived in the world to stop a hole, fill a lack. He seemed to be at one and the same time a phobic object and a counterphobic one for his mother. And so, when she saw that he was no longer playing this role, she attempted suicide, unwilling to consider treatment for herself at the time. As for Xénophon's sisters, why was it with him and not with them that the mother replayed her story? Or was the story replayed in a different way with them?

There are many questions that, of course, remained unanswered and that we must not try to answer by forcing them into a theoretical framework. This is always detrimental to an analysis, since clinical practice, contrary to what one too often hears, is not intended to illustrate theory. Theory, for its part, cannot explain everything, but it provides guidelines for treatment so that clinical work is not haphazard.

To conclude the discussion of the case of Xénophon, let me report a final enigma. In the last sessions the mother announced that she had been cured! After a long period of depression, she became well at the time of the suicide attempt. As she saw it, this was a miracle cure; she had no idea why she had been depressed from one day to the next or why she suddenly felt better. Of course, she said offhandedly, things were different now, since she was pregnant again. Her husband didn't know; he didn't want another child and would be furious, but he'd get over it. He didn't have to know everything, and she wouldn't tell him until matters became obvious, and then it would be too late. Throughout this session she emphasized the similarity between this pregnancy and the time she was expecting Xénophon. Everything was the same, nothing had changed, everything was in order again.

What she told me so insistently (and also defiantly) was proof that she had completely understood what had happened in her son's treatment. But, once again, she was unable to do anything except rig the game in advance.

16

Alice, or the Black Sun of Phobia[1]

It was September and Alice had just turned 7. She was referred to me by the doctor at the clinic where she had been seen for two years following several years of difficulty in nursery school. Alice's mother spoke of this failure in the first hour, and of another one, her new pregnancy. As Alice listened motionless and smiling, her mother spoke of how upset and desperate she was at finding herself pregnant again at 40; she was much too tired to bring a fourth child into the world. She felt depressed about the contraceptive failure and, at the same time, guilty about not wanting the baby. Alice kept on smiling. Her long blond hair tied in ribbons, her huge blue eyes, and the strange fairness of her skin made her look like a porcelain doll. She was absent, indifferent, and of a disturbing beauty.

The mother said virtually nothing about Alice's birth or her early months of life. She had forgotten everything with the ex-

1. An earlier version of this case discussion appeared in Mathelin 1993.

ception of one precise detail: she had conceived Alice on the day she had found out about her own mother's death.

At 3 months, Alice had been a baby with no problems— calm, quiet, never crying. She had had to be awakened for her bottles. At 9 months, after infections in both ears, she had had convulsions and was hospitalized for an evaluation. Normally such a good baby, Alice had had a dreadful time in the hospital; she refused food, cried, screamed, and was inconsolable. The parents were asked to come less often. The evaluation period was followed by surgery, and, when Alice's behavior remained unchanged, parental visits had been stopped completely. Alice had left the hospital a few days later. Her EEG was now normal, but she herself was not. She would cry when her parents came near her, would refuse her bottles, avert their gaze. Six weeks later, she needed to be rehospitalized for severe weight loss accompanied by dehydration.

Alice had been 12 months old at the time of the second hospitalization. She no longer cried, and would never cry again. She drank all her bottles and would remain motionless for hours. She began to walk at 2½ and said her first words, "Daddy" and "Mommy," at age 4. At 7 she was still not toilet trained.

While Mother recounted this history, Alice swayed gently in her seat, her back to me. Turned toward her mother, she fixed her eyes on the mother's mouth as if spellbound by the movements of her lips. Mother broke off her account and said, "Stop, Alice! Don't look at me like that; it scares me." Still staring at her, still smiling and swaying, Alice asked her in a mechanical voice: "It's raining? It's raining?" "Of course not, Alice. It's not raining," Mother replied. "Look out the window—it's sunny. It's really annoying how you always ask the same question." The mother went on to complain about how Alice persistently asked if it were raining twenty times a day without registering the answer. These were almost the only words she spoke at the time.

Alice had turned back toward me like an automaton. She looked out the window over my shoulder but seemed to see nothing there. She kept on repeating, "It's raining? It's raining?" I said, "It's sunny out, but maybe it's raining in Alice's heart? Maybe Alice would like to know if it's also raining in her mommy's heart?" Alice met my gaze for the first time. She rushed over to her mother's handbag and, in one movement, came back and emptied it violently at my feet. Then she flung herself toward her mother and pressed her head against the woman's stomach.

In the following hour I saw Father for the first time along with Mother and Alice. Alice remained seated, calm, indifferent, without reaction. Mother too seemed calmer and did not speak much in her husband's presence. They described their life as comfortable: they loved one another, loved their jobs, loved children in general and their own in particular, with perhaps a soft spot for Alice. At home they fought over who would get to hug her and offer her a lap to sit on. On this occasion they recounted a history that was smooth and tranquil, without suffering, just like the face of Alice, who listened, without blinking an eye, to a narrative as orderly as the ribbons in her hair, as the pleats in the little pink dress spread out around the child-doll.

And yet sometimes Alice would have terrible tantrums, would scream, bite, hit her head against the wall or the floor, rupturing the silence of the house. Father remarked:

> We're used to it. She gets into these little rages; it's nothing bad. Of course, we can't go out or plan the same vacations as everybody else, the same life as everybody else, but with understanding and love anything is possible. We're lucky people. We had happy childhoods, professional success, and wonderful children. Why should we be unhappy?

This question, which came like an echo to Alice's "It's raining?", was one that Father would often ask in the sessions throughout the following years.

At the end of this second hour I was alone with Alice for the first time. She seemed more worried. Seated on the couch where she had been while her parents were present, she swayed as she repeated, "See Daddy . . . see Mommy; see Daddy . . . see Mommy" like one of these modern dolls with a repeating tape inside them. I said, "You can open the door and see Daddy and Mommy in the waiting room, but here in the office, with the door closed, Daddy and Mommy can't see Alice." She quieted down and rushed over to the toy basket. She wanted to overturn it as she had her mother's bag; a puppet fell out and its head suddenly came off and rolled on the floor.

Alice then went crazy. She bit herself, hit her head against the wall, threw herself at me and scratched me, tore at her hair and mine. I took her hands firmly in my own and spoke to her over and over about her panic, about the horror she was experiencing, about her fragmented body and the volcano inside her head that was causing her so much pain. I told her that I would help her to contain her fears and her panic; just as I was holding her hands, I would help her to understand. She gradually calmed down, and the storm was over, leaving both of us exhausted. But, at the moment when I thought that she was finally hearing me, that a word had passed between us, and that what I said had enabled her to come back to herself, I realized that this was not the case. I noticed that her eyes were fixed on my lips, and that the movement of my lips was rocking her as if in a cradle, just as had happened with her mother in the first session. It was a desperate attempt at fusion on the part of a puppet who had lost its head. Alice had indeed quieted down, not because of what I had been saying to her, as I had hoped, but because of the movement of my lips: she had not come back to herself but glued herself back together.

It would be months and years before Alice could understand that lips said words that had meanings and were not just a cork stopping up her anxiety like an autistic object setting off an ecstasy that she constantly sought and that her mother could not tolerate.

In the third hour Mother came alone with Alice. She spoke once again about the wonderful childhood she had had. But her history, recounted with detachment, was full of the same violence as this quiet little girl. As in so many cases of autism, death was involved. One of her sisters, part of a set of twin girls, had fallen ill with toxicosis and had died "of neglect" at 6 months. Alice's mother had been 7 at the time, the same age as her daughter today. When it was clear that the baby was dying, her parents had gone away, leaving Alice's mother hovering over the crib, her gaze fixed on her sister. She had no recollection of how she had felt at the time, but she remembered the sister's convulsions and turned-up eyes at the moment of death, a moment Alice's mother had been awaiting, alone and terrified, for hours.

She recalled that her mother had wept and that she herself had experienced jealousy but not grief, since she was too young: "Children don't feel that kind of thing," she believed; what she had felt was envy. When her mother had been pregnant with the twins, she thought she was carrying a boy; in those days there was no ultrasound to determine the sex of a fetus. The birth of two girl babies had come as a complete surprise to the family. Alice's mother remembered being in the room where her mother had just given birth and having seen blood and also two very ugly babies in a cotton-filled box. Two girls. She had been filled with scorn for her parents: How could they have been fooled so easily? They should have brought back a boy from the market.

They must have been cheated by a dishonest shopkeeper who had given them two girls instead. So maybe they weren't so smart after all!

A month later, Alice's mother had surreptitiously taken one of the twins to a neighbor in the hope of exchanging her for a cow. The neighbor, amused, accepted the offer and told the story to Alice's mother's parents. They congratulated the child, saying, "That's a good idea you've got. We aren't very rich, and a cow would be a help. But we've decided to trade you instead of your little sister." From that day on, she became resigned to the presence of the little sister and said nothing more.

It was only after the baby's death that she became terrified of the idea that she could be exchanged for a cow. Even today she still saw, at night, her little sister's eyes during the convulsions, then Alice's eyes, and those of an injured bird that she had had to finish off, and those of the family cat, who had been epileptic ever since he was struck by a car. She was always the one who had to take care of people and animals in pain, always the one who had to do the dirty work. Alice's father was not always there. For years at a time he had had to work out of town. He had been absent during the year she was pregnant with Alice, and had not come back to Paris to work until his daughter was hospitalized. He had not come to the first interview.

Alone with Alice for the third session, I spoke about what her parents had said, recalling her history and her mother's and saying how hard it must have been for her to help a mommy who was so alone and unhappy. She got up and rushed over to the light switch. I intercepted her, saying, "There are other ways to be. Alice can't control everything. There are other ways to make the fear go away."

For the first time, Alice seemed sad. She took the toy basket and turned it upside down over her head. The shower of toys falling over Alice reminded me of her initial question; it was raining toys just as the contents of her mother's bag had rained down. Panic-stricken, Alice felt her body spilling out as the toys flowed onto the floor. I told her this. She calmed down and went over to my desk and took some sheets of white paper that she attempted to stick onto the window as if to block it; she then went to stick others onto the door, then came and sat down in the middle of the room, swaying. She was sitting cross-legged and smiling. At that moment my answering machine was activated and the noise alarmed her. She quickly got up and ran over to the telephone, but in her haste she ripped her dress. Once again she was in the grip of a terrible crisis, tearing off the garment that no longer protected her. Standing there undressed, Alice wept, real tears flowing down her cheeks. I spoke to her again, but this time I referred to her history and that of her parents. It seemed to me that she quieted down without needing to resort to autistic rituals. She was, however, in great distress, and when the hour was over she ran toward the door. I stopped her in order to say goodbye: "It's important for us to say goodbye to each other, Alice. It's because we leave each other with words and meet each other with words that people can keep themselves apart."

Rosine Lefort (1988) speaks of the anxiety aroused in a psychotic child, Robert, by the "loss" of a garment:

> Let us come back, then, to the envelope of the body, the apron, that, although it was imposed by the Other, had become so necessary for Robert that it seemed as though he would die if it were taken away. This apron was, apparently, an envelope like the membrane surrounding the child at birth, the child's first loss. Robert was thus completely alienated in the signifier "Madame," and the apron represented his Other; its loss was the loss of the Other. When this apron was sepa-

rated from his body, he was no longer "Madame": *jouissance* was unloosed from his body and went wild in terrifying, destructive crises in the absence of the Other. [p. 632]

The beginning and the end of the following sessions marked the establishment of genuine contact between Alice and me. I met a gaze that was different from her usual one; a frame could be constituted. The three initial interviews set the tone for the first six months of our work. For the most part Alice was mute and seemed to want to remain oblivious of my presence. Sessions in which she appeared transfixed and immobile alternated with violent outbursts that I was not always able to soothe.

At the end of out first year Alice began to quiet down. Because I spoke to her, put words to her fears, tried to contain the body that was spilling out into my office, and made constant reference to her experience, her anxiety attacks became less frequent and less systematic. She took great care in making sure that the door was shut, and this ritual seemed to calm her. It was at this time that she began to say a few words.

In the course of the second year Alice slowly became willing to enter into contact with me. At moments when she was not so scared, she spoke furtively to me. This was not the speech of the crazed child—incomprehensible words flung out in screams as if in another language—nor the stereotyped speech of Alice in her robotized states, but a different kind of speech. She took the risk of speaking genuinely while looking me in the eye, and the risk of hearing what I was telling her about herself and her history. It was as though a world in which ideas could exist were gradually coming to replace one in which everything happened through the body.

At the end of each hour Alice now said calmly, "Goodbye, Mathelin. Alice will come back." When a noise outside the office disturbed the session, when a drawer accidentally overturned

Figure 1

with a terrible crash, when a gust of wind blew open a window that was not tightly closed, Alice no longer bit herself, no longer screamed. She would sit on the ground, clutch her stomach, and say, crying, "It's raining. Alice stomach hurt," or "Alice scared."

At the beginning of the third year she began to be able to draw (Figure 1). There was never any scribbling; she drew forms from the outset. Forms "without eyes," she explained. In time there appeared a figure with a body, arms, and legs. In the fourth year the figures were given a mouth and, like Alice, began to be capable of true speech (Figure 2).

Figure 2

Outside of the sessions, Alice was making a lot of progress in her socialization at this time. Now that her parents saw that she was less anxious, they turned their efforts to teaching her. Since she did not have the feeling that she existed in her own right, however, she could learn only in the form of behavioral training. Her language use and vocabulary increased, but on occasion she reminded me of a ventriloquist's doll. She became toilet trained, she no longer ate with her hands, but she drew figures and houses that were entirely stereotyped and without individual character, exactly like the model she had been given. The school was astounded at her progress. Yet Alice was as absent in these drawings as she had formerly been in her silence.

In the sessions I had to struggle to keep the well-trained Alice from depriving the real Alice of life, to keep the tape recordings from covering over her own words.

During the fifth year she constantly repeated: "Alice isn't crazy, . . . Alice isn't scared." But her eyes, which were no longer inexpressive, still revealed horror. Her "adaptation" was serving as an autistic technique. Just as there were two kinds of discourse at home, she made two kinds of drawings in the sessions. Some were stereotyped and mute, the sort she had been taught to do; the others were the ones we worked with. We set those of the first kind aside, and Alice decided that they were for Daddy and Mommy. The others stayed in my office and were for her. They were mostly shapeless and terrifying.

One day she drew a kind of rectangle. "It's a box," she said, "a box with a wolf inside." To one side of the box she drew an odd moving body and explained: "That's Alice. The wolf is very scared." Of course the wolf was no match for her—nothing could be scarier than Alice's body (Figure 3).

At this time in the analysis, the family's epileptic cat died with the help of Alice's mother, who explained that he had to be

Figure 3

put out of his misery. Alice went through new anxiety attacks during which she seemed to be imitating epileptic fits. Her frightened mother blamed herself for having put a sudden stop to all the progress Alice had made. I spoke with her, in the child's presence, of these dramatic repetitions, of the burden of death in their history, of the little sister and the crises of Alice, the bird, and the cat.

At this point Alice, who was drawing more and more in the sessions, seemed to begin to try to construct an object. She drew monstrous cats who scared her so much that she had to stay under the table for several minutes after each drawing, so that she wouldn't have to see the cat (Figure 4).

At the same time, the parents reported the outbreak of a cat phobia in her. These cats, she reported, were named Alice. She identified with the dead cat, just as her mother, in a complication of the oedipal process, had identified with what had seemed to be most important to her own mother, namely the

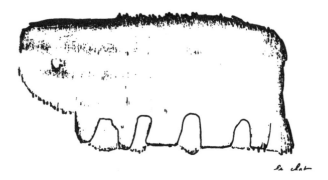

Figure 4

little dead sister "in a hole," as she put it, a hole in which she too wanted to disappear.

In her sixth year of treatment Alice was unable to touch the modeling clay and wasn't interested in the toys, but she drew and described her drawings. One figure predominated: the snowman (Figure 5). Asexual, neither girl nor boy, fragile

Figure 5

and without substance, the snowman could slip between one's fingers like the water of which it was made. It could change form if it melted. This figure clearly expressed Alice's feeling of physical vulnerability, of a body that, no sooner formed, might vanish with the first ray of sun. Its inside and its outside were identical. Perhaps even more archaic than fantasies of the body in pieces, it seemed to represent Alice's feeling about herself.

If sunlight came into the office, she asked that the curtains be closed before she would draw. Whatever the form of the snowman, even if it were no more than a puddle of water, she always gave it two eyes, two holes that she colored black. "It's the eyes that are scary," she said. "Not the snowman. The eyes are inside its head." "Inside Alice's head?" I asked. "Daddy's and Mommy's eyes are inside Alice's head," she replied. From this time on, Alice would ask me about whether her head, her thoughts, and her body were transparent, and with great anxiety she described the person who spoke inside her head. Projected onto the snowman, the all-powerful gaze seemed to turn away from her somewhat.

The parents now indicated that Alice was beginning to be frightened of dogs. This was a dreadful fear: Alice, who had never been afraid of anything except herself, now would risk getting run over in the street if she saw a dog on the sidewalk. She added that she was afraid only of small dogs. At the same time as she developed this phobia, the wolf returned in the sessions, but this time it was a frightening wolf, a disturbing one, who confronted an Alice whose body was that of an amoeba (Figure 6).

One day she drew a wolfhound (Figure 7). "It's the story of the wolf that scares Alice because she was afraid of the dog," she explained. "It looks like." "Looks like who?" I asked. "It looks like it looks like. When Alice is afraid of the dog, she isn't afraid of the cat and she isn't sick anymore."

Figure 6

In this way she explained how her cat phobia had been dis-placed onto dogs. And indeed, she now feared only dogs of about the same size as a cat! Large dogs did not bother her; it was only small ones that she wanted to strangle.

From that time on she included in each of her drawings a circle colored black, like a black hole, another version of the snowman's eye, a flash of emptiness at the top of the picture. This is what enabled her to draw. She explained that this is what scared her like "the eye of the dog or the mosquito who sees

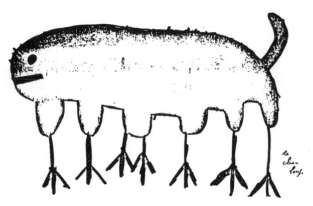

Figure 7

everything." This hole was a "don't know." She drew what she was unable to say: this not-me black hole, these devouring monsters who were not tamable and who were one big gaze like the people who spoke inside her head and whom she could now put in the drawing.

Once the black hole was in place, Alice felt able to draw herself (Figure 8). Now she knew what she was afraid of. The fear was circumscribed and the phobic mechanism seemed to make it possible for Alice to exist. She learned to read and write with her parents, but the shape of the word was more important to her than its meaning.

Like the black hole, the figures she drew were surrounded with reassuring garments, containers without contents, enclosing the unspeakable horror of the body. When I asked Alice, "Who's this?" she would reply, "It's a skirt," or "It's a dress," "It's a coat." The figures became actual people later on, but the black hole remained, as if to make the drawing possible. By now

Figure 8

it had become a black sun, one that was frightening but at the same time watched over the people in the picture (Figure 9).[2]

Like many autistic people, Alice was an object of horror to herself. More precisely, she was not phobic about herself—which, in her case, would not have meant much—but she had a phobia about her own body. Does the autistic child's horror of her body serve to keep mother at a distance? Or does it reflect the dreadful despair of a mother whose child evokes no feeling, the impossibility of the reverie of which Bion speaks, the vertigo of a mother who cannot imagine her child? Who becomes the phobic object of whom? Figure 10 shows what the mother–child bond was like for Alice: an umbilical cord hanging by a hair, yet the two people are welded together. The child's face is a blank, an emptiness.

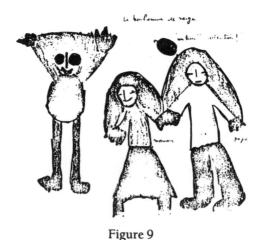

Figure 9

2. Translator's note: The figures in the drawing are labeled, from left to right, "the snowman," "mommy," "daddy." The dark circle is labeled "a hole—watch out!".

Figure 10

Whereas her mother experienced an inner upheaval, Alice was able to project the horror onto an external object—the wolf, the snowman, the black sun—just when the mother was beginning to look elsewhere, differently.

Lacan (1968–1969) describes phobia in these terms:

> It is in regard to phobia that we can see something that is not at all a clinical entity but is sort of a turntable. . . . This is not something that can be isolated clinically; it is rather a representation that is clinically illustrated in a way that is certainly striking, but in infinitely varied contexts. [Personal notes]

It may be said that Alice was able to emerge from autism thanks to this turntable that is phobia, or, to use a more exact metaphor, by the construction of a phobic object that was a true lifesaver for this troubled child. Alice was at this time struggling with the constitution of the object, an object that had hitherto coincided with her. She was the "cork child" of whom Frances Tustin (1991) speaks:

In certain circumstances, a mother may unwittingly use her infant as an inanimate object—as what McDougall calls a 'cork child'—to fill the hole of her emptiness and loneliness. In my experience, such a mother is under-confident and/or bewildered and/or deprived and/or depressed, or she may have experienced a shock, tragedy, or bereavement around the time of the child's birth. [pp. 586–587]

An autistic child, as Alain Vanier (1993b) explains, serves as an object to stop up the mother's anxiety: "It can happen that the child fills this gap to overflowing. In autism, the object provides total blockage. It is not taken as a semblance; it is the object that completes the fantasy of the other, and the subject can identify with it" (p. 33).

Did Alice have a choice whether to be something other than the beautiful doll-object? Colette Misrahi (1991) gives a precise description of Sophie's anxiety when faced with her inanimate doll:

Through the doll, Sophie grasped the difference that marks the inert and the animated, machinery and life. That was the source of the stupid things she thought up with regard to that enigmatic and ambiguous being: under the repeated assault of Sophie's brutality, the doll remained mute. In the silence of the doll, was there not some *jouissance* hidden? [pp. 50–51]

Wasn't Alice an enigmatic and ambiguous being for her mother? A fetish-child? Perversion might also have been a way out for her, but this child knew only fear and absence. The void protected her from despair; the less fearful she was, the more she would be able to feel grief.[3] Her mother's history and her own, including the dramatic experience of her hospitalizations (which, we may recall, had affected her ears), had prevented her from hearing the meaning of words, from building an inner life for herself that consisted of something other than death, pain, and chaos.

In connection with the case of Robert presented by Rosine Lefort, Lacan (1953–1954) emphasized the importance of the sole word used by that child: "the wolf" was what distinguished him from a savage; it was as if, from deep within him, Robert were calling to be inscribed in the symbolic order:

> In this very special case, we see, embodied there, this function of language, we touch on it in its most reduced form, reduced down to a word whose meaning and significance for the child we are not even able to define, but which nonetheless ties him to the community of mankind. [pp. 102–103]

Robert began to form a concept of the law around this pivot of language. For Alice, the only connection to the world, the connection that contained all her meaning, was her persistent question: "It's raining?" "It's crying," children say when rain falls.[4] It was raining Alice, this child who spilled over and emp-

---

3. Adrian, an 8-year-old autistic boy, confided to me after a long analysis that he felt sad because he was making progress.

C.M.: Why does that make you sad?
Adrian: When I make progress, I fall.
C.M.: You fall?
Adrian: Yes, I fall in love. It makes people unhappy when they love you; I don't like to see Mommy cry.

4. Translator's note: *il pleut* ("it's raining") and *il pleure* ("it's [or "he's"] crying") sound similar in French.

tied herself out. A mass of objects rained from her body and from her mother's bag, but none of them had thus far enabled her to construct herself, none was truly "Other." These objects were merely "others" that did not even make it possible for her to weep. When her father did not inscribe himself in the place of the Other, when nothing could be transmitted by the mother and the Name of the Father remained foreclosed, the oedipal law could not make itself heard by the child. Tustin (1991) notes that, in cases of autism, fusion with the mother entails a lack of influence on the part of the father; since these children do not have the experience of sharing the mother with the father, their omnipotence is unchecked, and under their passive appearance they can be willful and dictatorial.

When Alice established a phobic object for herself, she was attempting to enact the triangular oedipal drama. As with all phobic objects, hers was set up in the father's place. But this was just an attempt. There was finally a sun for Alice, yet it was black. It was black, yet there was a sun. This was the trap in which she remained caught (see Figure 11).[5] Alice's psychic structure was neither neurotic nor perverse: it remained psychotic. There was surely no father in the handbag emptied out in the session.

Xénophon's treatment (see the previous chapter) shows how the issue of the construction of the object was framed differently in his case. At age 7 he did not speak. He screamed all day and, in terror, avoided making eye contact—indeed, any sort of contact—with others. This clinical picture had led the consulting psychiatrists to make a diagnosis of autism.

But when we follow the course of the sessions, it is clear that Xénophon was much more present than Alice, so present

---

5. Translator's note: The caption on the picture reads: "The man on the boat, he's afraid of the sea and the waves. The sun is black."

Figure 11

that he constantly felt that he had to flee. He could not speak, but he could already draw. His body was not his sole means of expression; he did not bite or mutilate himself. When he had an anxiety attack, he would hide under furniture in order to get away from an other (who was thus already there), to escape a gaze that existed outside him and not, as with Alice, inside his body. When he began to talk, even if in a fearful whisper, he used complete sentences. The words were available and had a meaning. He was afraid of everything, but his body was not a phobic object; the phobic object was already outside him. Certain phobic patients have what Tustin (1972) calls an autistic shell, but the object has been constituted and they have access to speech, access to the father. This was not the case for Alice.

In her reflections concluding her presentation of the case of Robert, Rosine Lefort (1980) says:

I can't say whether my desire reached the borders of the Other of the Law for Robert. Strictly speaking: yes; but there remain the unresolved questions of the transmission of this desire to the psychotic and the proof of the reducibility of the foreclosure of the Name of the Father. Lacan did not believe—and we agree—that this is possible (which did not prevent him from affirming without reservation the urgency of taking psychotics into analysis). . . . At the least, Robert escaped the fate of being confined to an institution. Our experience has shown that, for certain psychotic adults, analysis was able to avert the solution of a delusional reconstruction of the world by maintaining or reestablishing a relation to an Other that did not entail the permanent destruction of their body. [pp. 643–644]

Alice is now 20 years old. She seems fairly well adapted to the world, and she has given up autism. She is able to live in society, and her behavior is such that she has been able to begin training for a career. But, after twelve years of analysis, one morning when she was quite sad, Alice, who did not know sadness, said to me: "Alice doesn't like you, Mathelin. You've made her too unhappy. Now Alice will never be able to be the way she used to be."

17

Jeremy, or the "Clown Theater"

I first met Jeremy in a context of violence. I was waiting in my office for a child who was to come for his initial appointment, when the concierge of my building rushed upstairs breathlessly to ask me to respond to an emergency. A crazy boy was shouting in the courtyard, threatening everybody and breaking the tiles in the entryway. The janitor had tried to control him, but the boy had kicked him in the ankles. The mother was shouting that she had an appointment with me, and the janitor was going to call the police if I didn't come at once. "Really!" said the concierge. "The other evening a woman screaming on the stairs, and then that man who rang all the doorbells, and now a destructive child! Having a psychoanalyst in the building is like letting the devil into your house. Take care of him, but go by yourself, because I'm not going back there." So I left my office and went alone to meet the devil.

He was a tall boy of 8, with huge blue eyes, who seemed frightened and dreadfully unhappy. He was breaking the tiles in the entryway and shattering the respectable order of this quiet building with his cries. His mother stood beside him, weeping. Looking out from their balconies, the neighbors commented unfavorably on the scene. I approached him and tried to speak to him. I told him who I was and that he had an appointment with me, that I didn't want to keep him from being angry, but that he'd be better off telling me about himself in my office, since what he had to say was no one else's business. To my great surprise, he agreed to follow me, but he still did not stop shouting.

On the doorstep Mother explained that he had been yelling ever since they had gotten out at the station and seen a fire-eater in a carnival. "He's always been very afraid of fire," she said, "and of storms and fireworks." I led him into my office while he repeated over and over, "I'm scared of the man spitting light." I closed the door and tried to quiet him down: "The man can't come in here. We can't see him, and we can't see the light." I drew the curtains so as to screen the July sun that filled the room, and the semi-darkness seemed to reassure Jeremy.

He gradually became calmer. Sobs still shook his chest, but his eyes were dry. He stopped shouting. I then tried to explain how the circumstances of our meeting were such that I knew nothing about him. I hadn't had the time to speak with his mother, or to try to understand anything other than his panic. I had had to try to contain my own panic—not to mention making a phone call to the police, who had been alerted by well-intentioned neighbors, to persuade them not to come. "What a funny way for us to meet, Jeremy!"

Jeremy looked at me in surprise, his eyes a transparent blue. He began to smile and went to the desk to take felt-tip pens and paper. "Wait," he said. "I'll tell you about the fire." He took a pen in his hand and began to cry: "No, no, Jeremy can't draw." He held out the pen: "You do it, you do it."

I took the pen and asked him what he wanted me to draw. This was the first time a child had asked me to draw for him, but in Jeremy's tears I had understood that I had to accept a task that at this time he found impossible. It was a question not of drawing for him but of letting him make use of my drawings. His anxiety was too great, and I had to go along with him.

"Draw a house without a roof, and a man; you do it." As I drew a house without a roof, I wondered at this odd choice of words. He seemed satisfied and commented on the picture:

> The man got lost. He couldn't find his house, because he had an accident. His car broke down and went right into the water. There's a clown in the water. He was laughing, the clown. He has a red nose. Bang!—he got hit. He got lost in the pond. He's dead, he's not well. He has ice on top of him.[1] There were too many accidents. They had accidents before him, and now he can't escape. It's all screwed up. The car went splash from the accident, the light, the fire, the smoke.

Jeremy looked up at me and began to shout again: "Don't put on your glasses! Take them off! Take them off!" I did so. "There!" he said. "I told you about the clown. Now I'm going. That's all." Only after many more sessions did I realize that everything *was* really there in this first hour. But on that day all I could see was the fire and Jeremy's fear. I told him that and asked him whether he wanted me to speak with his mother. "No, no, not Mommy. I don't want her to look at him." He became very anxious. "She not look at him, no, no!"

The easy option would have been to bring Mother in, but I sensed that doing so would compromise my work with Jeremy.

---

1. Translator's note: *Glace* means "ice," "mirror," and "sheet of glass."

"Will you come again, so that the two of us can try to understand about the man and the clown?" "Yes," Jeremy said. "I'll come again." Leaving the office, he passed in front of the mirror in the corridor. He stopped and seemed overcome: "Look at my clown." In a state of great excitement he jumped up and down, laughed, waved his hands in front of his eyes, and shrieked, "Look at him, look at him!"

Hearing the noise, Mother came in from the waiting room and Jeremy suddenly froze. "Not you. Not you." He threw himself down on the ground, kicked her, and began yelling again. "No, no, don't start that all over again," his mother begged. He got up, opened the door, and pushed his mother violently. Over all the racket she shouted, "Did you make another appointment for him?" I had. He left, taking his mother and his clown with him. As the door closed behind them, I stood there dumbfounded and disconcerted, understanding nothing of what had just taken place.

When he returned for the second session, he was calm. Mother was visibly relieved that he had made it to my office without difficulties in the waiting room. Upon entering, he said, "Take off your eyeglasses. You're the one who's going to draw." Again he asked me to draw a house without a roof, and a man:

> The man's lost in the ice. The cars are in the ice, like the ice of eyeglasses, and they can't get out. Look at my feet! [My desktop was made of glass, so he could see his feet underneath it.] Look, they're in prison under the ice also. The man is lost; he has no house; he doesn't talk. The clown threw him in the ice. Great big eyes are looking at him.

He glanced at the window and began to moan, "Close the curtains—they mustn't look." I drew the curtains and asked who it was who mustn't look. He answered in a whisper, "The spider's eyes. They're as big as mountains. The spider comes at night. It's poisoned. Big as a man. See, it's the clown who threw the man in the ice to get revenge." "Who is the man?" I asked. "It's the other one. The clown is in the water, in the speech-ice, and he can't move, can't talk; he's not allowed to leave."

C.M.: The speech-ice is like a prison of words?
Jeremy: Yes. He would have to live in speechland. But there he can't speak. He's all screwed up. That's all; I'll come back. What about Mom?
C.M.: She's in the waiting room. Last time you didn't want me to talk to her.
Jeremy: I don't want her to come.

He came back to the desk and turned the drawing face down. I said that perhaps he didn't want her to see or hear what went on in the office. He nodded, and so I suggested that we meet her in the waiting room. He happily came and led me to the door, putting my hand on the knob. When we got to the waiting room he sat down and immersed himself in a book. Not once during the interview did he look up.

Mother reported that Jeremy was 8, and that he was in the second grade in a Montessori school but, according to his teachers, was not even functioning at first-grade level. He disrupted the class with his unsettled and aggressive behavior, was always clowning around, laughed for no reason, and waved his arms and legs around wildly like a disjointed puppet. He made the other children laugh and usually refused to take part in activities, including drawing. The principal did not think she would be able to keep him in the school.

He was desperately afraid of light and fire. At age 2 he had been labeled autistic and then (since he spoke rapidly) psychotic, on account of all his quirks, of the way he moved his hands, shouted for no reason, and said he was afraid all the time. He did not answer questions and did not react appropriately, or even comprehensibly, to people and things. He was frightened, and he was frightening to adults, who dared not let him out of their sight and were at a loss as to how to calm him down, reassure him, or simply persuade him to please stop yelling.

Jeremy's mother had been in analysis for two years. She said that she now understood how difficult things must have been for Jeremy when he was born. The year before, she had had a premature baby, also named Jeremy, who had lived only a few days. The second Jeremy was conceived, according to mother, on the very day on which the birth of the first one had been expected: "It was just one eighteen-month-long pregnancy for me," she said.

Jeremy number two was born at term and in good health. He was a very quiet baby, with no problems apart from some difficulty in finishing his bottles. "It used to drive me crazy. He always had to be coaxed, but he was all I had, and I had eyes only for him." Jeremy was 1 year old when his mother became pregnant again. She recalled that she was happy with this third pregnancy, that she was at last recovering from the death of the first Jeremy and was no longer afraid; she knew that another child would be good for both of them.

In the third month of the pregnancy she was alone in the house with Jeremy when she had a miscarriage. In her panic she phoned the police, who rushed her to the hospital. She took Jeremy along, since she could not leave him by himself at home. He screamed, it was nighttime, there was the screaming of the sirens, the lights, and a mother who was too anxious herself to be able to soothe him. The mother saw this as the origin of Jeremy's withdrawal into himself, his cutting himself off from the world. At this time, too, Jeremy's father asked for a divorce and left Paris. She had lived alone with the child ever since.

A kindergarten teacher, she managed to keep Jeremy in her class for three years in a row because of his problems: "This child needed constant supervision; another teacher wouldn't have been able to stand it." She now wanted him to be in analysis too, in order to "help him live." Jeremy, hearing his mother crying, took his nose out of his book. He nestled against her and said, "Mustn't cry; the man fell into the ice; mustn't cry."

"You see," the mother said, "he always talks nonsense." Jeremy thereupon got up, rushed into the corridor, and flattened himself against the mirror. "Look at the clown; look at the clown," he said with a desperate expression. At that moment I realized how unbearable things were for him, how he was shipwrecked and drowning in the mirror. I went and stood between him and the mirror, between him and the image of the crazy man. With my back to the mirror, I faced him and prevented him from seeing the clown in the ice/mirror. Astonished, he stopped gesticulating and asked, "Where's the clown?" He no longer looked anxious but seemed quite intrigued.

I replied, "The little boy I see in front of me is Jeremy. He's 8 years old and he doesn't talk nonsense." He left, looking serious, lost in his thoughts. From then on, for five years, Jeremy's sessions were less violent. He came quietly and agreed to let me speak regularly with his mother, but only in the waiting room. As for the father, he came only two times, but these were two very important times for Jeremy.

The first two sessions were spectacular—they were presented as performances to be seen. Jeremy set the stage and brought on the actors. In the foreground was the clown imprisoned in the ice/mirror, the clown who prevented Jeremy from recognizing himself when he looked in the mirror and prevented him from having a name. There was no access to the symbolic in that mirror; there was just the imaginary.

His mother was undoubtedly too stupefying, like a narcotic that paralyzed him. Looking at her, he could not encounter the other who would look back at him. She did not allow a different gaze. He could see only the Jeremy of his nightmare, a prisoner in a glass cage, his nose injured from being knocked against the glass in his attempts to escape: the brother, or rather the double, who had become a poor disjointed clown through metaphoric sliding.

To look at a mother who was looking elsewhere would have alienated him, but would at the same time have permitted him to find himself. As it was, he was abandoned to the ghost and the unnamable and could not succeed in "making himself":

> Thus this *Gestalt*—whose fullness of meaning should be considered to be bound up with the species, though its motor style is still subject to misrecognition—by these two aspects of its appearance symbolizes the mental permanence of the *I* at the same time as it prefigures its alienating destination; it is still pregnant with the correspondences that unite the *I* with the statue in which man projects himself, with the ghosts that dominate him, and with the automaton in which, in an ambiguous relation, the world of his own making tends to find completion. [Lacan 1949, pp. 2–3; translation modified]

The clown is simultaneously a threat, for he can attack, and a victim of accidents that preceded him. This clown takes revenge by luring the "man"—that is, the boy—into the prison of the mirror, where death imposes silence. Because I blocked the clown, severing Jeremy from his mesmerizing image, the second Jeremy was finally detached from the first. I named him, I told him that his words had meaning, and he calmed down. It was as though he had to be protected not only from his own gaze, but also from the gaze of the lethal spider—the *jouissance* of contemplation, the absolute gaze, devouring and possessive, that endangers the child. Jeremy staged a terrifying spectacle, and he replayed it over and over again. He occupied the empty place, filling the lack of his depressed mother who had no words to exchange, no other interest beyond this child and the care she had to give him. "[T]he satisfaction of need," says Lacan, "appears only as the lure in which the demand for love is crushed" (1958, p. 263).

In the tenth session Jeremy got angry when, as usual, I was drawing for him: "But that's not how the man looks! I didn't want him to have clothes on! Why did you make him with clothes on?" I explained to Jeremy that things would be much easier if he himself drew whatever he wanted, since I couldn't know what he had in mind, and, although he told me what to do, my picture would never be exactly what he wanted. If he drew, he would be the one to say how it should be. For the first time Jeremy took the marker from my hand and drew a man (Figure 1). He told the following story about the picture: "It's still the man who's the prisoner of the ice/mirror. The clown is also there. There was a very big storm with fire and light. The lady, not the daddy, prevented the little boy from being crushed. It's very cold in the ice/mirror." I asked: "What's in the ice/mirror?" "You know what's there," Jeremy replied. "That's where they bury children."

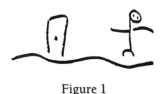

Figure 1

During the first year of analysis these themes persisted. The "man" and the clown were prisoners of water/ice/glass. It caused nosebleeds if you bumped up against it trying to get out; the clown's red nose was the sign of that injury. There were always cars, accidents, and houses abandoned after the accidents.

At the beginning of the second year I saw Jeremy with his father. Father said that he didn't see Jeremy often because he felt very guilty for having "abandoned" his wife. He also spoke about his first son, the other Jeremy, about whom he often thought. If the baby hadn't died, perhaps he and his wife would not have separated.

While his father was speaking, Jeremy drew a different picture, not his usual one (Figure 2). There were two houses (one of them with a roof), a pond, and a man who seemed to be holding one of the houses, the one without a roof, so that it wouldn't collapse. Jeremy explained:

> There was a big storm near the house. The daddy and mommy found the man. There was a storm and a light. A lady came into the street to save the man who was being crushed by the mommy, but someone kept him from being crushed. The little boy was saved. The clown stayed in the ice/mirror. His nose got redder and redder. He bumped it. The little boy is saved from the ice/mirror.

Figure 2

In the fourth year of the analysis Jeremy's father came for a second appointment. But after the first one he had resumed contact with Jeremy, writing to him and phoning him more often. He even had him come for fairly regular weekend visits. After that first appointment Jeremy had made real progress in school; he learned to read and write and to solve math problems. "Before, he never used to understand what he was supposed to do," his teacher said.

Was it in the play about the two houses, which went on for some time in the sessions, that Jeremy was able to bring onstage one house from before father left and one after? One house with "you" and one without?[2] One with triangulation, the other without; the one that no longer had a "you" had to be held up by him in his identification with the cross in the cemetery. "Look!", Jeremy said smiling. "He's got a cross-body." A cross-body sacrificed to the *jouissance* of the other. Perhaps without him, without his support, his mother would really have died?

Some months later, at the beginning of an hour, Mother told me that Jeremy was very upset because the husband of a babysitter he liked a lot had just died in a brutal way. Jeremy said:

> He had whiskers. The doctor took care of his nose but he went away to the ice/mirror; no, to heaven. Why can't people go to heaven? Daddies and mommies cry when they bury their boy in the ice. Do you know when you're going to die? When Jeremy is going to die?

When would Jeremy finally die! I spoke to him about his dead brother. He drew the clown (Figure 3). "This is a clown," he said, "who catches all the bad things. The man doesn't catch

---

2. Translator's note: *Toit* ("roof") and *toi* ("you") are homonyms.

Figure 3

them, but he catches worries and he's afraid of falling in the ice/
mirror." After this session Jeremy no longer stopped in front of
the mirror in the corridor. He simply said, each time he left, "The
clown is there," but he no longer needed to be the clown, since
he was now truly separate from it.

Jeremy, overwhelmed, went to the funeral of his babysitter's
husband. At the cemetery he asked to go to his brother's grave;
he had never been taken there before lest he be traumatized. For
Jeremy, the babysitter's husband was really dead and buried. He
understood for the first time that the man would never return.
In this death the real, the symbolic, and the imaginary were inter-
mixed. His "uncle," as he had called him, was resting in peace.
He was no longer a prisoner of the mirror. Before the burial Jeremy hadn't been sure of this, but finally he accepted it.

Each advance in this child's treatment seemed to be connected, not to interpretations, which were apparently useless,
but instead to the staging of what was going on in his interior
theater, his extraordinary fantasy life. The same play, each time
it was repeated in every session, was no doubt what finally enabled his story to be inscribed and to take on meaning. It took

years to play out the theme of the clown and the man, to clarify
the meaning of the sheet of glass that had to be broken through
in order to escape from the world of the dead, and to put a stop
to the metonymic sliding of ice, water, and mirror in which Jeremy had become lost. He staged his story (for it is not the analyst who is the producer of the drama), anchoring himself in the
transference session after session so as to be able to write his
theory, his own myth.

After four years of analysis, and in the wake of the father's
second appointment, Jeremy undertook more oedipal themes.
The drawings remained the same: a house, a "man," a pool, but
now with the addition of a robin. This bird kept watch above
the house; Jeremy explained that it chased away the "man"/boy
who wanted to be at peace in his own home with his gleaming
treasure and his mother. The robin was in fact "a cutthroat[3] who
keeps everybody from doing what they want. The boy and his
mom," Jeremy went on to say, "are afraid of the cutthroat robin.
He doesn't want him to come. The "man" wants to kill him. Go
away! Go away! It's very dangerous and makes moms cry. Dads
have spankings in their hands when the boy wants to shout."

Jeremy's mother was the one who always accompanied him
to his sessions. She did not say much about herself, since she
was in her own analysis, but she reported a lot about her relationship with Jeremy. In spite of her own suffering and anxiety,
she got to the point where she could let him go away for a vacation with some friends of the family, far from her supervision.
She gradually regained her self-confidence. Jeremy was now in
junior high and working at grade level. She began to hope that
he might be cured.

---

3. Translator's note: *Rouge-gorge* ("robin redbreast") sounds like *coupe-
gorge* ("cutthroat").

In the last year of the analysis, the "man" came alive in modeling clay. Leaving at the end of the hour, Jeremy would adjust his bowtie in the mirror. He could find himself in the mirror at last, assume an image: "We have only to understand the mirror stage *as an identification*, in the full sense that analysis gives to the term, namely the transformation that takes place in the subject when he assumes an image" (Lacan 1949, p. 2).

The "man" got ready for a long voyage to a faraway country. Aided by a siren with magic powers, he built a wondrous boat. The voyage would be long and very dangerous—an odyssey. Preparations were often interrupted by fearsome enemies who had to be fought off; the journey, once the boat was on the water, would be full of perils and traps. But the "man" continued onward and could no longer go back. Jeremy explained: "An old woman said to a child, 'I don't want to see you here anymore; you're grown up and it's time to leave.' The boy wants to go to the village of men, the country called speech."

But the path was long and difficult.

In the final scene of the final act Jeremy became anxious: "Over there, there's a terrible light and a storm. Over there, it's the village of men. There's a dad who says, 'Come on, it's fun in the village of men.'" When the curtain fell Jeremy turned to me mischievously and said, "Do you remember when I was afraid of his light?"

Part III

The Clever Baby

The same soul rules both bodies. . . . .
The things desired by the mother are often
marked on the limbs of the child she is
carrying at the moment she desires them.

—Leonardo da Vinci

18

A Look at the Baby of Today

"Ernest is apparently much more talented in modern jazz than in classical music." Mrs. B, four months pregnant, made this statement in all seriousness. She had just begun teaching her son music by a new Japanese method based on recent scientific findings to the effect that a fetus becomes able to hear in the fourth month of gestation.

But wouldn't it have been somewhat inappropriate to speak of Ernest as a fetus in front of Mrs. B? His sex, height, weight, and name had been determined, pictures of him had been distributed to friends, and on Sunday afternoon, between the slides of their last vacation and the videotape of their nephew's skiing lessons, his parents had shown the cassette of Ernest's ultrasound.

Babies aren't what they used to be! In former times all we could do was imagine them, fantasize about them. Nowadays scientific progress has turned our romantic reverie into knowledge that claims to be true. If it has been proven that the baby hears us beginning in the fourth month of intrauterine life, we, for our part, can see him. This gaze may be innocent, moved, annoyed, or perverted, but it may also be scientific. In this last case, there are prerequisites: the eye must be that of a scientist, which (according to other scientists) guarantees that it will not be innocent, moved, annoyed, or perverted. The experimenter being, by definition neutral and impartial, does not feel; he looks. He must efface himself in order not to invalidate the experiment.[1]

This scientific gaze is called observation, and its technique, enormously successful ever since the 1970s, is on its way to supplanting all others. Some behavioral psychologists use this approach to explain away analytic theory as a Freudian delusion, a groundless construct. Well accustomed to this type of argument, analysts are hardly swayed by denunciations of the paucity of scientific "evidence" furnished by psychoanalysis. They are more likely to be amused when this topic comes up.

A trickier matter is the analytic approach to experimentation. For it is the case that some analysts of established reputation, no doubt intoxicated by the same dream as Freud, the dream of finally making psychoanalysis more scientific, would like at all costs to reconcile observation and analysis, to ground psychoanalysis in scientific laboratory experiments, to make observation into an analytic technique and a method of treatment.

Though observation has always been present in treatment, it is caught up in the transference. Up to now analysts have never been researchers, and their desire has never been confused with that of observers. Freud often noted that analysis could be known only through "hearsay": from his early studies on hysteria onward, the emphasis was always on hearing and not on looking. The frame of the treatment and the recumbent position of the

---

1. On these very grounds of impartiality, the eye of the camera is often preferred to the experimenter, who is there only to decode image by image.

analysand favor openness to what is not seen, to the invisible, to what could get free of the image and the imaginary. The observer, in contrast, privileges the scientific gaze. The camera replaces the eye because it is more "neutral"; for the same reasons the two-way mirror is preferred to the physical presence of the researcher in the room. Slow-motion and freeze-frame techniques are used as a kind of behavioral microscope to see what the naked eye cannot see. Nothing must escape the researcher in his attempt to see better and further.

But the analyst, for his part, attempts to hear beyond words. This is such a different register that the two approaches cannot be reconciled. Taking note of behaviors and quantifying them, effacing subjective parameters and singularity, avoiding as far as possible the personal influence of the researcher that would distort the experiment—this is an approach that runs counter to that of the analyst. As Alain Vanier (1992) notes:

> What observation . . . wants to eliminate as an artifact is the presence of the psychoanalyst. Yet this presence is not what contaminates the situation to be observed, but instead perhaps exactly what structures it. Winnicott's (1941) paper on the observation of infants demonstrates how such observation is valid only in the context of the treatment. The analyst is irretrievably involved in it, and what is therapeutic in this work is that one leaves the field open for the entire course of an experiment. [p. 25]

But even beyond the problem they pose for analysts, mustn't we fear that the recent discoveries concerning the abilities of the infant, of what Freud called His Majesty the Baby, will plunge us into a period of pedagogic madness? An unleashing of the imaginary, a heightened narcissistic reverie—this child who yesterday could do nothing is now said to be all-powerful. Ever since scientists, our modern storytellers, have leaned over the cradle, we have learned that babies see correctly (Fantz 1963); their focal distance is good and, from birth on, they are able to pursue objects visually and fix their gaze on them. We also know that they hear and that they can single out their mother's and father's voices from those of other people. MacFarlane's (1975) experiment shows that babies have a sense of smell, being able to recognize a piece of cotton soaked in their mother's milk. And they show a preference for some stimuli over others. Sherrod (1981) demonstrated that they look more attentively at symmetrical figures (like the human face?); they are thus capable of differentiation. Numerous studies, most often American, show in a rigorous manner that the newborn is capable of concentration, of surprise, and of learning.

Eliacheff (1993), in her book on psychoanalysis with very young children, mentions an experiment dealing with their ability to learn rudimentary calculation. No one, to my knowledge, has yet proposed to see whether babies can learn to read, but the Japanese are testing their ability to learn foreign languages! Filming the expressions of babies while doing concurrent electroencephalograms, the neuropsychiatrist Boris Cyrulnick (1991/1993) has shown that infants smile even in the delivery room; he explains scientifically that the first smile is determined by a neuropeptide, a bioelectric brain secretion.

And yet, is there any memory more intense than that of the moment when, finally in its mother's arms after the tumult of birth, the baby smiles at her? What is happening at that moment—a secretion of neuropeptides? Certainly, since science demonstrates it. But nothing more? Can this "remainder" be quantified, measured, registered on an electroencephalogram? The remainder is precisely what psychoanalysis has set about to investigate. Do we have a technique to measure desire? Confused, with no sense of what they are doing, researchers attempt to track down thought. On the lookout for the very first signs, they descend on babies right in the delivery room, not to welcome them, but to evaluate what they can do without really caring about what they are. As Catherine Dolto-Tolitch (1990) has observed, the general level of health in our culture is not so high that we can afford to welcome the majority of infants into the world with so much violence, so much disrespect for the persons they already are and will become. Such a dehumanizing reception can warp development, leading to neurosis, perhaps even psychosis, in any case to distress.

What exactly do scientists want? Does the all-wise baby reflect an image of adults unable to understand everything, alienated, subjected to desire, to speech, to the imaginary? Researchers have gone as far as to assert that the baby's wisdom derives from his very inability to speak. According to Daniel Stern (1985), the acquisition of language, the difference between life as lived and as represented, alienates the child and causes it to lose some of its abilities; while language enhances the apprehension of reality, it also, paradoxically, distorts the experience of it. Before speech, in this view, there is a "true self," after it a "false" one. But, a Lacanian would ask, isn't it language that is structuring, that creates the subject, even if the price to be paid is alienation?

What is it that, in the adult's fantasy, the preverbal baby knows all about? The surface of an ideal projection, isn't what this baby knows our own repressed knowledge of sexuality? Ferenczi (1955), observing that in the course of analysis his adult patients often dreamed of scholarly babies able to speak, write, and give scientific explanations, notes that the manifest content of such dreams recalls the lament of the libertine that he did not make better use of his infancy! According to Ferenczi, what is at issue here is actual knowledge of sexuality, familiar to the child but later permanently buried when repression becomes operative. Isn't this something we need to keep in mind today more than ever?

This raises an important question about the impact of experimentation on the child. Observation of cognitive capacity necessitates the infant's being subjected to testing situations designed to measure its ability to discriminate colors, to orient itself in space, to recognize geometric figures, and so forth. But the experiment becomes more complicated if what is to be evaluated is what the child feels, its adaptation and attunement to its mother. The notion of attunement, introduced by Stern, is rather hard to define. Here is the sort of experiment that illustrates it:

> The approach of creating defined perturbations in naturalistic or semi-naturalistic interaction is well established in infancy research. For example, the "still-face" procedure [of Tronick and colleagues] asks a mother or father to go "still-faced"—impassive and expressionless—in the middle of an interaction, creating a perturbation in the expected flow. Infants by three months of age react with mild upset and social withdrawal, alternating with attempts to re-engage the impassive partner. [1985, p. 149]

Another experiment involves asking a mother, previously instructed as to how to "perturb the structure" of the baby, intentionally to misjudge the child's degree of animation in the course of a play session:

> When the mother [jiggled the baby] somewhat more slowly and less intensely than she truly judged would make a good match, the baby quickly stopped playing and looked around at her, as if to say "What's going on?" This procedure was repeated, with the same result.

> The second perturbation was in the opposite direction.
> The mother was to pretend that her baby was at a higher level
> of joyful animation and to jiggle accordingly. The results were
> the same: the infant noticed the discrepancy and stopped. The
> mother was then asked to go back to jiggling appropriately,
> and again the infant did *not* respond. [pp. 150–151]

For all this to have any scientific value, the experiment had to
be repeated a number of times, and, to be sure, the baby no longer
responded.

In *La Cause des Enfants* [*In the Interest of Children*] Françoise
Dolto (1985) is strongly critical of the researcher Herbert Mon-
tagner in connection with an experiment he performed on
nursery-school children, the point of which was to demonstrate
that in the most tense of the children their mother's odor produced a regression and a withdrawal from play. An undergar-
ment of the mother's was hidden on top of the cupboard in the
classroom. Why, Dolto asks, given that the result was predict-
able, was this potentially traumatizing experiment, this frightening manipulation, necessary, making guinea pigs of vulnerable children? Whenever there is experimentation on human
beings, she states, one must above all be certain to do no harm
or else to abstain.

Isn't this dogged scientific hope that everything can be explained in the laboratory even more imaginary than the fantasies of our grandmothers? Non-knowledge is not the same as
ignorance. And are the discoveries made on the basis of such
experiments essential for the understanding of the human being?
In a talk given in 1953, Jenny Aubry overturned the received
ideas of the time by showing that babies suffer, that they experience with great distress deficiencies in maternal care. In those
days there was scarcely any interest in babies; children were
believed to experience no psychological problems until the age

of 4 or 5. It was clinical experience, not scientific experimentation, that supported Aubry's demonstrations. But if we turn to Stern's *The Interpersonal World of the Infant* (1985), we learn that sophisticated research allowed him to show that there is no such thing as normal primary autism—is this a revolutionary advance in analytic theory? The critique of the existence of a phase of normal autism in the infant was made by Jacques Lacan in his 1975 Geneva lecture on the symptom. There is no mother–infant symbiosis, since from the outset there exists a third term, a lack on the basis of which all interaction is organized. How can we imagine a scientific protocol to discover lack? As Faladé (1987) observes: "Before the child is born and sometimes even before its conception, before it cries or speaks, it is spoken about. There is already *alienation*; something of the parents is already there that will mark the child if it comes to be born" (p. 49).

The old notion of normal autism denounced by Daniel Stern seems to be more particularly linked to trends in America associated with Margaret Mahler's (1968) belief in an omnipotent, hallucinatory psychosomatic fusion with the representation of the mother during the first weeks of life. In England in the 1960s the situation was different. Winnicott (1975) was critical of the concept of symbiosis. The mother had to be "good enough"; a too good, symbiotic mother was dangerous. When the mother, responding to the demand for the good breast, gives the infant the belief that it has created the breast, this is merely an illusion. And Winnicott knew that this could not be proved by filming that illusion.

Another English analyst, Frances Tustin (1972), likewise sharply criticized the concept of normal primary autism, seeing autism as a reaction to the trauma of physical separation, not as a regression to an allegedly normal developmental stage. Here too, how could one film what clinical experience taught Tustin,

Lacan, or Winnicott? According to Tustin, the infant experiences the nipple as a part of its own body, not the mother's. Autistic children suddenly and traumatically lose control of what they feel to be a vital and essential part of their own tongues, a part that gives them the feeling of being alive. When the nipple part of their tongue is not there as soon as they need it, they experience the black hole of non-being. On a film, even in freeze-frame or slow motion, all we will ever see is a breast belonging to the mother and a child with an empty mouth or a full one. The child with a breast-mouth as described by Tustin and Lacan, and the mother with a hole in her chest, can never be represented objectively on even the most sensitive film.

The uniqueness of analytic theory lies precisely in its rootedness in clinical experience, that is, in the transference. Isn't scientific illusion just another way for analysts to protect themselves from transference? A little common sense never hurts, even for scientists. We must follow Françoise Dolto's advice concerning this type of research and ask ourselves whether we would do likewise with our own children.

19

Cannelle and Gingerbread: A Child Who Looks Good Enough to Eat

The night was dark, the forest deep and dangerous when a man and his wife, poor woodcutters, decided to take their children, Hansel and Gretel, far away from their cottage and abandon them. After three days of walking, the lost children, exhausted, hungry, and trembling with fear, discovered a delightful house made of cakes, candy, and sugarplums. Filled with wonder and certain that they would finally be saved, they drew near and found inside the house an old woman. Despite her kind appearance, this old woman was a wicked witch who was on the lookout for children and had made her little gingerbread house to attract them. When a child fell into her hands she killed it, then cooked and ate it, and this was a holiday for her.

Witches have red eyes and they don't see well, but they can sniff things out as well as animals can, and they sense when human beings are approaching. Seeing Hansel and Gretel, the witch gave a wicked laugh and cried, "These two won't get away!"

C. M.: "Do you know the story of Hansel and Gretel?

Mother: "Yes, ever since I was a little girl. I used to think it was a little like my own history. I even hung a drawing of the candy house over my bed. I remember how hard it was for me to be an only child. Gretel was lucky to have Hansel to protect her; I was abandoned to the witch.

Cannelle[1] had been referred to me by her pediatrician. Her parents quickly set up an appointment and arrived, distraught, with their baby. As they entered the office, Cannelle was already crying in her mother's arms.

Father: You see? No need to explain—you know why we're here; you just have to have ears. We can't go on like this. She's 3 months old today, and she hasn't stopped crying. All day long, all night long, it's awful! She hasn't slept since she was born.

As I sat in wonder, Mother went on:

Mother: She sleeps, but never for more than a quarter of an hour at a time. Every night she wakes up and cries. Every quarter hour, since she was born, we have to get up and give her the pacifier, then she sleeps for another quarter of an hour and begins to cry again. We can't take it any more!

Father: We're exhausted. The pediatrician advised us to send her away to a children's home for awhile. It's quite a distance from Paris, but if she doesn't quiet down by next week we'll take her there and leave her.

---

1. Translator's note: "Cannelle" means "cinnamon."

This turn of phrase reminded me of the strange atmosphere of fairy tales.

> *Mother:* We wanted this baby so much, we love her so much, but we can't stand her anymore. We just can't live with her, understand her. Maybe she doesn't love us? But we show our love to her; every day we eat her up with kisses. It's a terrible thing to say, but we're going to wind up strangling her if we stay with her.
>
> *Father:* The pediatrician advised us to see a psychoanalyst before placing her in the children's home. You never know—apparently even very little babies sometimes have funny ideas. It's strange, especially since according to him she's perfectly healthy and has no problems.
>
> *C. M.:* What was the pregnancy like? And the delivery?
>
> *Mother:* It was a wonderful pregnancy. We'd been wanting a baby for such a long time but couldn't conceive. We'd already been married for seven years and I was afraid it wasn't possible anymore. She was nearly strangled during the delivery, but it turned out fine in the end.
>
> *C. M.:* "Strangled." That's the word you used when you were saying that you couldn't stand her anymore.
>
> *Mother:* Oh, that's just a figure of speech. The doctor said that the cord was wrapped around her twice. In the maternity ward, the first day, she suddenly began to scream. The nurse was quite sure that it was because the gingerbread man had scared her, so it was thrown away.
>
> *C. M.:* The gingerbread man?
>
> *Mother:* It's a long story.

C. M. (*to Cannelle, who is still crying*): Listen, Cannelle, Mommy is going to say something to us. If you make all this noise, we won't be able to hear what all three of you have come to tell me today.

Cannelle looked at me for an instant and resumed her crying, her head turned toward her mother's breast. The mother continued her story, raising her voice in order to be heard despite her daughter's distress.

Mother: You see, talking to her doesn't do any good. Maybe we don't know how to take care of her. My stepmother says we're too young, too inexperienced. It's our first child, and we're just twenty-five.

C. M.: Your stepmother?

Mother: My father's wife. She brought me up; my mother died when I was 3. I was alone with my father, and he got married to my stepmother a year later. I was 4 and became anorexic. I didn't like her, and I think I was trying to annoy her by refusing to eat. She loved to cook. She would have done anything to win me over, but I knew that she wasn't really interested in me. She stuffed me with candy, cakes, and gingerbread. I adored gingerbread more than anything else. She made it for me because that's all I would eat, but even though she did all these nice things I hated her.

　　I still remember how violent my hatred was. One day I got sick and had to go to the hospital because of all the sugar I'd been eating. The doctors put me on a diet. When my father came to see me in the hospital, he brought me a rag doll he'd made for me. He called it "the gingerbread man." I remember how much I loved it. When I was scared at night I'd fall asleep sucking on its hands.

One day—I was 8 or 9—my stepmother threw it away; she said I was too old for such a silly thing. We never got along. She even stopped pretending to care about me. There was open war between us, and my father was at his wit's end. Our relationship is still a difficult one. I got married so young in order to get out of the house.

I really don't know why, but when I found out that the baby was going to be a girl I sewed a gingerbread man for her out of brown felt. It looked exactly like the one I used to have, but it must have been too big for her. I'd put it in her crib. Do you think it frightened her?

Father: Of course not; what a question! She's just throwing tantrums, that's all. She's like that because my wife's too gentle, too nice. If she listened to me, there'd be no problem. She's too anxious. She's always afraid the baby's going to die and she holds her all day, so the baby doesn't want to be in a bed anymore. She doesn't want to be alone; she's been spoiled and that's why she cries all day and all night. I'm sure that the children's home will do her good. It's terrible. I realize when I listen to my wife that I can't reassure her.

Mother: I couldn't bear for her to leave me now. She's just 3 months old; she's so little.

I then spoke to Cannelle, who, in her mother's arms, turned toward me when she heard my voice and stopped her crying a little. "So, Cannelle, you hear what Daddy and Mommy are saying? You've been crying ever since you came out of mommy's belly, ever since you've been able to make noise, as if you were afraid that no one would remember that you exist. But you're there!"

Cannelle opened her enormous eyes. She seemed curious and interested and looked at me with remarkable attention, her mouth wide. "Well, Cannelle," I said, "if you're afraid of Mommy's fear I can understand how you don't want to sleep." Cannelle stared at me wide-eyed, gazing at me with extraordinary intensity. She had stopped crying, but now it was her mother who was crying silently; big child-tears flowed down her cheeks as she looked at her daughter.

> C. M.: Don't be afraid, Cannelle. You can sleep. Mommy can sleep at night, too; you don't have to cry in order to cure her fear. It's as if you want to reassure her all the time, to shout to her that you're alive, to tell her that you won't leave her alone the way her mommy left her alone back then.
>
> Mother: Do you think it's the gingerbread man's fault?

What did she mean by "fault"? How could I answer such a question? Once again I spoke to Cannelle:

> C. M.: You see, Cannelle, there's Mommy's gingerbread man and there's Cannelle's. I'm not at all sure that I agree with the nurse that yours is what made *you* afraid. Gingerbread is part of Mommy's story. What she gave you is a different doll. It certainly looks like the first one and has a lot in common with it, but it's not the same. You don't have the same father and mother as Mommy. She made it for you, for your own story, which won't be the same as hers, even though you're her daughter.

This new voice gave Cannelle an alternative, another path. She seemed to swallow my words with her whole body, and while her mother continued to weep I kept on telling the baby about the mother's fear that she was trying to exorcise every quarter hour with her crying. Suddenly the child's eyes turned up, her fists opened—and Cannelle fell asleep. The parents were stunned: "She's never gone to sleep like that!" She slept right through the hour, and even when she was being dressed to leave she did not awaken.

> *Father:* I think she'll sleep for a long time now. She was always so tense that she has to recover.

When they returned the following week for their next appointment, Cannelle was no longer crying and was able to sleep, but the parents complained that they had been fighting all week long. How can we understand what was going on with Cannelle and her parents? Do we have to understand?

In his seminar on transference, Lacan (1960–1961) has this to say about understanding:

> It isn't absolutely essential for him [the analyst] to understand. I'd go as far as to say that, up to a certain point, his not understanding is better than his being overconfident in his understanding. In other words, he must always place what he understands in doubt and tell himself that what he's trying to reach is exactly what, in principle, he doesn't understand. Of course, it's only in so far as he knows what desire is, but doesn't know what this subject, with whom he has embarked on the analytic adventure, desires, that he's in a position to have within him the object of this desire. This, it seems, is the only way to explain those kinds of effects that are so exceptionally alarming. [p. 229]

To understand is to be caught up in the demand of the other; it is one of the ways of responding to that demand. But demand is not desire.

If, as Lacan has taught us, it is important that the analyst not seek understanding at all costs—for this would turn him into a doctor or scientist and would make it difficult for him to stay in his role—we must nevertheless consider the effects of speech in analytic work with children who, though caught in language, are not yet able to talk. It is clear to those of us who work with very young children that, even if we don't always understand what is going on in the session, babies do "understand" what is said to them. Clinical practice with infants seems to offer fresh proof of this every day.

After several sessions, they regain their appetite or the ability to sleep, or they are cured of somatic illnesses for which medical treatment was of no avail. In the mystery of the encounter with babies, we are called upon all the more to work with what we do not understand. The results, often spectacular, perplex the analysts themselves; they don't want to be taken for magicians, since, depending on the times, the shadow of the stake can pose more or less of a threat.

As matters now stand, no scientific explanation can tell us whether a baby of 3 months can understand an interpretation. As Catherine Eliacheff (1993) has observed,

> With regard to the domain considered the most advanced among cognitive sciences, namely language, we are—at least for now—far from wanting to verify experimentally the structuring value of the truth of their lives as we express it in words to children, something that psychoanalytic observation confirms every day, although we don't know how. Despite rapid and astonishing progress in neurobiology, this discipline does

not enable us to answer the question: How can human beings who have not yet acquired language understand? For that matter, we do not know how, in adults, certain words can lead to distress, heart attacks, or accidents, even if we are coming to learn how speech affects the biology of a human being, which is not the same thing. [pp. 64–65]

In this session with Cannelle, one thing was certain: this was not observation of a baby. I even had the impression that it was Cannelle who was the observer. Her attention was exceptional. There was nothing experimental in this encounter, nothing measured, foreseen, or controlled. Although the analyst seeks to guide the interview, he does not seek to dominate it.

What word was the effective one, and for whom? Something undoubtedly happened for all three, parents and child, or else Cannelle would not have been able to sleep and the parents would not have spent the week fighting. The father had mentioned that it was impossible for him to calm the mother and the child. Neither a reassuring brother Hansel nor a father who could compete with the "gingerbread man," he left his wife and daughter in the grip of the witch. The mother seemed incapable of finding soothing figures except in an incestuous relationship. She hadn't married early because of her husband, she said, but to escape from her family. There was no place for a man chosen to be her own.

This "no place" (in which the mother's father was perhaps complicitous) became apparent to the husband in the course of this session. And how can we determine exactly what went on for the wife, overwhelmed by a session during which so much of her history had been discussed? What she reported in the following hour is entirely typical of the kind of work that can be done in an initial session with a baby and its parents.

> *Mother:* When I left last time, I felt lighter. Cannelle didn't feel so heavy in my arms, and then, especially, I don't know why, but when you said that her gingerbread man wasn't mine, I felt relieved, as if you were saying that Cannelle has a different life from mine. That evening I gave her back her gingerbread man. I think that she's not scared of it anymore, and that she can love it.

Cannelle needed to be relieved of this mother's very weighty history. Had the mother ever mourned her own mother? What terrifying love story still bound her to her stepmother? Why did she live in fear of her baby being taken from her? Fantasies of retaliation? Repetition of the drama of her mother's death? How can a baby whose mother is afraid it will die at any minute live in peace?

No doubt she was afraid that, once she became a mother, she too would disappear. A little girl's enormous love for another little girl devoured by kisses,[2] a baby with a sugary name, rich with the sweetness that she had missed so much when she herself was a child, to the point of getting sick and needing to be hospitalized, fantasies of devouring, death wishes, desire for life—all were part of the cannibalistic violence that formed the relation of Cannelle and her mother. In this mirror relation neither could sleep, and both wept, wore one another out, and sustained one another without its being possible to tell which kept the other from sleeping, while the father remained unable to set

---

2. "Children before the age of two . . . confuse hugging with a bit of cannibalism. They think they are being eaten" (Dolto 1990, p. 113).

a limit to the the horror of this *jouissance*. The two sessions seem to have loosened this enmeshment somewhat and to have enabled Cannelle to find her own history and her own place.

But this symptom removal, however comforting to the child and the family, solves nothing. Once Cannelle had been "cured," her parents did not want to return for further sessions. Isn't this one of the effects of "magical cures"? No wonder analysts are never truly satisfied with them.

20

An Analyst on a Neonatal Unit: "A Different Experience"[1]

Physicians seem to be making more and more room for analysts on their services, especially in the area of early childhood. Having an analyst on call is becoming the latest "must" in advanced medical technology: "Put a shrink in your incubator" is the current fashionable slogan in the treatment of premature infants. But, although we observe that nowadays the doors are open and the analyst is being called upon, it remains to ask just what it is that he is being called upon to do.

What do these doctors want when they turn to us? And what do analysts want when they venture into this galley-slavery, given that it's so much more comfortable to stay in one's armchair?

---

1. My work on this service was made possible by a team, all of whom, from the baby-tenders to the physician-in-chief, were animated by genuine concern for infants and their families. We all wish to thank Catherine Dolto-Tolitch, who for the past two years has spoken at a number of meetings and shared with us her experience with newborns. She brings to her teaching a "color" that is uniquely hers. Her syntheses were of great value for the team, as her colleagueship and her friendship are for me.

Some even believe that, beyond a certain distance from couch and armchair, one is no longer an analyst. Indeed, it is often the case that nowadays those of us who work in medical settings are more severely criticized by analysts than by physicians.

Yet we hear of psychoanalysis in hospitals as far back as Anna Freud's time (A. Freud and Bergmann 1945). Much ground has of course been covered since then, but do we really find it easier nowadays to work without running the risk of being reduced to the role of just another health care provider, of being hijacked into a situation incompatible with analytic work?

It all began six years ago, the day when the director of a neonatology service called the child psychiatry clinic at which I work and asked for a psychoanalyst. I was transferred to the service of Dr. Retbi at the Delafontaine Hospital at Saint-Denis, where, with the help of the team, I tried to establish an analytic practice quite different from the usual sort.

The general situation on most neonatal units is that a "shrink" is called in when parents decompensate, that is, when they present undue problems for the team. In such a case a consultation is recommended, if not actually prescribed, and the parents are usually followed in an office separate from the service, sometimes over a period of years, well after the child has left the hospital. The analyst is often unfamiliar with the baby's chart and does not seek contact with the medical team. Why not? This is a way of working that places the demands of the team in the foreground. Parents who interfere with the team's work are referred to analysts, who are asked to help the doctors out, though their task is obviously to look after the parents.

I found it impossible to work this way. I did not want to see parents who were already distraught and unhappy, and who, moreover, felt that they were considered to be in need of psychological services when they knew quite well that others who are "healthy" (or, rather, who do not bother anyone even if they are suffering terribly) are never summoned to see the analyst. So I tried to envision the work differently; something else had to be invented. This certainly wasn't easy, but the transfer had been made and the team wasn't putting obstacles in my way.

The issue was this: Could an analyst do what was required by the physician-in-chief and become an integral part of a highly technical medical service? To be on the team and yet separate from it in an analyst's role, at the same time present and detached?

Most of the demands of the service seemed to me to be compatible with my own professional guidelines, and so I agreed to assume this position with an orientation that recentered the work on the child. With unity of place as in Greek tragedy, I would be within the service. And there would be unity of time— the work would occur during the time the baby was in the hospital—and unity of action: my work, too, would be that of resuscitation or reanimation, but in a different register.

What was to be reanimated was the child's desire, connected to its parents' desire, in tandem with the reanimation of its body. "Reanimate" comes from the Latin *animus*, "spirit," "breath." Medical attention provides the breath of life, which is essential. But if medicine can put air into the lungs, speech can sometimes revive the will to live. When I talked with Françoise Dolto about this project, she summed it up as follows: "You are offering the heart that is a heart the wish to live, while the doctors are forcing the heart that is a piece of meat to continue to beat."

This is how the team functions today. The service is in an isolated place entered through two airlocks. A place within parentheses, between life and death, it calls to mind a submarine in the depths, far from the hospital that is its home base. Upon leaving, both children and medical personnel carefully go through stages of progressive decompression. The newborns who enter always arrive in a state of emergency, and each such arrival plunges the service into silence. The greater the emergency, the more slowed down seem the movements of the medical team.

At the time of admission, the supervisor sets up two appointments for the parents, one with the doctor, one with the analyst. The former is in charge of the child's medical care and reports to the parents on its state of health. He also confirms the second appointment, with me, and presents me as in charge of the baby's emotional development while it is on the service. The parents know that they have been called in not because they have problems, but because the appointments are standard procedure for all admissions. For the parents, this sharing of responsibility between the doctor and the psychoanalyst sets the work in an entirely different perspective.

In the first session, I explain my role with regard to their baby. It often falls to me to speak of the child when the parents themselves are no longer able to. The discrepancy between what I have to say about the baby and what they have heard from the doctors often surprises parents. I do not discuss the child's weight or its platelet count; instead I talk about its smile and its birth, about what I know of its history, of the words that seem to bring the child back to life in the parents' imagination and make it more human despite the horror of the real that they confront. When they risk taking their turn to speak, what concerns them is not knowledge—at any rate, not the kind of knowledge that doctors have—but the truth of a story: "I know he'll be all right," or "I knew when I was pregnant, even if everyone said everything was fine, I knew that the birth would be difficult."

The important thing is not to be outside the team but to be outside medical discourse.

Often parents ask about what they believe to be "the doctors' secrets": "There's something they're not telling us." These parents in effect know that something is unspoken, but they don't know that the unspoken is not necessarily on the part of the doctors. The answer is always disappointing. Why did this child die suddenly? Why was this baby premature? Doctors respond as scientifically as possible, in terms of their medical knowledge. The parents understand or they don't. We have learned from Ginette Raimbault (1976) that to answer only on the level of the organ is to answer only on the level of the symptom. No wonder parents are convinced that no one has addressed their concerns.

The analyst is there to insist that the answer is elsewhere. If we can endure not to attend to the parents' anguish in our answer—to put a bandage on their wound, as it were—the unconscious can risk appearing, and the parents may perhaps hear their question in a different way.

Much can be said in an initial meeting. A year after the death of his older brother, Paul, from sudden infant death syndrome, Frank was born. He was on the unit for the assessment routinely undertaken in such cases. Frank's mother lay siege to the doctor's office: "Why did Paul die?" she asked over and over again. Medicine had no answer. Frank was doing well, she was told; she should try to forget and not be worried.

When I saw her, she complained about the medical team: "The doctors say they don't know, but I know they're not telling the truth." She continued: "I had problems with Paul; he made me violent, but I loved him." She then went on to speak of the accidental death of her little brother, Pierre, who had fallen from the arms of her older sister. Their mother had been depressed for two years after the loss of Pierre, and there had been another little brother, born right after Pierre, who had never spoken: "He never got over Mom's sadness, and we didn't want to take care of him; I think we just let him drop."

This first interview, the only one because the baby was in the hospital for a one-day assessment, enabled this mother to weep and to glimpse the traps of repetition that lay in wait for her child. Her son Frank had been produced "on doctor's orders" to cure her depression; her family kept on urging her, "Now you don't have to be sad, because there's Frank. No one cries when they have a healthy child." She did not want to be depressed like her mother, and she did not want to drop her son. It had been impossible for her, until now, to speak of her unbearable depression and of this mourning that replicated another mourning that she had been likewise unable to experience. I referred her for a course of therapy with Frank, and the baby was gradually able to give up the "high risk" status he had been labeled with during his mother's pregnancy. But the risk did not stop there.

Much can be said in an initial meeting. At this time I explain to the parents that I will see them as often as they wish during the hospital stay of their child, in the office or in the ward along with the baby. A demand can be formulated from this time on: I will see them only if they request an appointment.

Only the first interview is systematic. I meet the babies at the time of the visit by the entire team. The medical history is reviewed and therapeutic decisions are made then and there on the basis of the baby's condition. The baby is discussed but not spoken to directly. It has been examined beforehand, and the visit proceeds with no lingering at the patient's bedside. What I learn on such occasions is valuable, not only so that I can understand what the parents tell me and how they have imaginarily shaped what the doctors say in order to make some sense of the inhuman reality, but also with regard to the children themselves, when I return to the ward to meet them individually. This other visit, or this visit "in another way," is one I make alone in order to talk to the baby about itself, its parents, its medical problem, the proposed treatment, what I know of its history. The medical personnel on the team, rather intrigued by all this, gradually began to follow me and to ask the same kinds of questions. Being an analyst on a medical service means being involved in the questions of a team, which is not the easiest thing in the world; the possibility of working as an analyst sometimes hangs by a thread. Or, to put it in other words, it's like walking a tightrope. From one day to the next, the support of the team may be withdrawn and can never be counted on to continue.

In this second kind of visit we speak *to* the baby, not *about* it. Previously the baby was observed; now the very fact that it is there concerns it. This story, as dramatic as it may be, belongs not only to the doctors, but to the child as well, and the child must play its role.

It is very important to let the parents speak of violence and hatred, and to do so to the child. Comforting words and good advice can soothe burning wounds temporarily and can reassure the caregiver, but they are superficial ploys that sustain the lie and thus risk a violent return in the life of the child. The story of Agnès is an example of such a mistake.

Born after thirty-four weeks of gestation, Agnès had spent two months in a hospital for premature infants. When she was referred to me she was 23 years old and had just given birth to an enchanting little girl weighing seven pounds. While in the maternity ward, this young woman experienced such severe postpartum depression that she had episodes in which she lost her identity. On the third day after giving birth, she escaped from the ward in an acutely confusional state, asking passers-by where she was. Hysteria? Hallucination? Postpartum psychosis? The hospital psychiatrist mentioned several diagnoses and referred her to me after prescribing medication.

"I'm seriously ill," Agnès kept repeating, and nothing reduced her to tears more than the well-meaning consolations of her family. Her health had always been excellent. An easy child to raise, she had posed no problems until now. Adopted into a family as a baby right after she left the hospital for premature infants, she knew virtually nothing about her birth mother, the social service department at the hospital having revealed very little to the adoptive parents.

These parents were seen by a psychoanalyst in the hospital; they followed his advice carefully and concealed nothing from their daughter. Thus from a very young age she knew that her given name had been chosen by her mother, who had come to see her regularly during the week after her birth. But before being discharged from the maternity ward, the mother had said she wanted to place the baby for adoption and had disappeared, leaving the social service worker with a false name and a false address. Nothing else was known, except that she had been considered to be quite ill while in the hospital, though no precise information about the illness was forthcoming.

The adoptive parents, on the advice of the psychoanalyst, had told Agnès everything they knew and even what they didn't know. Their primary goal was to cast the relationship in a positive light. Thus they told her that her abandonment was an act of love on the part of a good mother to whom the adoptive parents were very grateful. They said this, but thought otherwise. The error was due not so much to the advice of the analyst as to the parents' misunderstanding of the violence of an adoption.

This "soft" version of the facts convinced Agnès, who, to the great satisfaction of her parents, grew up with no problems. Upon learning shortly after her marriage that she was pregnant, she was very happy. She awaited the much-wanted baby in an atmosphere of joy, delight, and mutual understanding with her husband and her family. The pregnancy progressed without complications, except perhaps for a few difficult days after she had learned from the doctor—whom she described as a magician "who can see inside the belly"—that the baby was a girl. She was glad, yet found herself troubled without quite knowing why. Three days after the ultrasound, she had an episode of uncontrollable vomiting. Nevertheless, she thought that "it'll be sweet to have a little girl."

The only hitch was the baby's given name. She had chosen boys' names but could think of none for girls. The vomiting stopped when she suddenly thought of the name Marie-Agnès, and, over the protests of her family, who saw in this choice a lack of imagination instead of a search for origins, she remained firm in her decision, and eventually things returned to their normal, calm, happy state.

At the end of the seventh month contractions began. Agnès was hospitalized; the doctors felt that the baby was too small and prescribed rest and an IV. Agnès tried to refuse, saying that she wanted to give birth prematurely. As she put it, "I felt that this was the moment of her birth; I don't know why." Her family and the doctor reasoned with her, and Agnès, who from a very young age had always been extremely reasonable—never any anger, always very positive—finally gave in. She agreed to rest without further opposition. She seemed no longer sad, but perhaps a bit absent—resigned, no doubt, to being misunderstood.

After several weeks the baby had reached what the doctors considered normal weight and treatment was discontinued. Five hours later Marie-Agnès came into the world via a normal delivery. Everyone was happy with a task well done. But for three days Agnès declared herself too tired to hold her daughter in her arms. By the third day she no longer knew her name nor why she was in the hospital.

What emerged in her analysis were horror, hatred, and violence concerning her birth mother: "How could she have abandoned me? Now that I've got a child of my own, I know that
she's a monster." What monster was she talking about? Who was
whose monster?

The hatred had been covered over by the good intentions
of adoptive parents, who had been counseled too well. Torn apart
by ambivalence yet rejecting it, Agnès wanted to proclaim in any
way possible her connection to her sick mother, a mother with
whom she could identify only as monstrous. After a period of
analysis in which she rediscovered the drama of her history and
came to see the meaning of the symptom "threat of premature
birth," she was able to take back her daughter, for whom the
grandmother had once again become an adoptive mother; this
was a history that could only keep on repeating itself as long as
it was not understood.

It isn't easy to avoid stepping out onto the slippery slope of
the wish to cure. The task of an analyst on a neonatology service is not to reassure or to try to allay suffering at any cost. He
must accept and understand, or else twenty-three years later the
baby in the adult will relive the violence of a trauma that had
been denied. The unconscious can be counted on not to forget.
The apparent cure that one can bring about in no way guarantees the future of the subject. The analyst's role is difficult to
maintain, but this difficulty is not the result of working on a team.

Is it possible for a psychoanalyst to find a place in a technical team on a pediatric service? What is it that the parents want?
And can we speak of wanting on the part of the child? The only
clear demand with which it is possible to work is that of the team,
and, moreover, there is the question of the analyst's desire. When
all the doors are open, isn't there an even greater risk of being
hijacked, of being tempted to add to medical knowledge a kind

of psychoanalytic knowledge that has nothing to do with knowledge of the unconscious?

How to work in the camp of those who know, who have put on the white uniform of knowledge, without forgetting the more modest position of one who has everything to learn from the patient? The distinctiveness of the analytic task is not always made easier by the urgent demands of medicine.

Recently a mother told me that, when she took her hemophiliac son for his appointment with the hematologist at a large Parisian hospital, she was surprised to find that she was interviewed not only by the familiar doctor but also by another man, unknown, likewise in a white coat, who had been introduced neither to her nor to the child. The mother had at first thought that he was an intern, since he wore the white coat. But clothes do not make the man, and the supposed intern, as the mother was buttoning her five-year-old son's shirt at the end of the examination, told her that the boy could do this by himself and that her overprotectiveness was surely a sign of anxiety that could be very harmful to her son. As she stood in astonishment, since he hadn't been introduced to her, he told her that he was the psychoanalyst on the service. Perhaps we should say "the analyst on duty," as with a fireman in a theater!

The mother had asked, in amazement, "Is it really the usual thing for an analyst to say things to you like that without having been asked?" To which he had replied, "But Madame, it's in your interest and in the interest of the service." Whose interest was in question here? Why does medicine call on psychoanalysis to such an extent?

Admittedly, it isn't easy to be a physician nowadays. Doctors are confronted with complex problems: test-tube babies, anonymous donors, frozen sperm, miraculously resuscitated children who remain, in their parents' fantasy, children of medicine to the point where they are sometimes even given the doctor's name. It isn't easy to wield the kind of power that science confers. In the coming years, doctors may well encounter demands such as: "I need a little girl with blue eyes, to be born on Christmas day. I know your scientific knowledge will provide this."

The medical act is now situated in a domain different not only from that of psychoanalysis but from that which it occupied in the days when the medical was associated with the religious, the sacred. Today medicine derives its authority from science and deals with the "scientific" body, not with the body of desire and pleasure. Science does not give meaning to the symptom. The further medicine advances, the more it excludes the libidinal dimension of the body, which is not to say that we should forego therapeutic progress. But medicine links up with science in a problematic way. The object of medicine is a subject, and he forbids this. It is when they have to deal with the reactions of subjects that doctors who see themselves as scientists find themselves at a loss.

So it was in the story of Estelle, a 28-year-old woman seven and a half months pregnant with her first child. An ultrasound revealed that the baby was no longer growing; no cause was apparent and the doctor, worried, decided to keep Estelle in the maternity ward without offering her any explanation. The physician-in-chief uttered his verdict: "Your baby is big enough now and would be better off in an incubator than in your stomach." Because a placental abnormality was suspected, a Caesarian section was performed and a healthy five-pound boy, Sylvain, was delivered.

Estelle had come for a routine ultrasound. With no account given for the necessity of the intervention, she awoke five hours later, alone in a room, her stomach flat and painful.

Her baby had been transferred to the neonatal unit of another hospital, and she was not allowed to see him for a week while she was in the maternity ward. What reality could this child have for her?

The day finally came for her to be discharged. Her husband came to take her to see her son, but at the last minute she refused. The doctors did not understand; they had saved her baby and now she was getting depressed. What they of course could not understand (nor was this their role; if they understood, they might be unable to see) is what Estelle told me when she finally arrived at the neonatology unit, still unable to go near the incubator.

In session after session, Estelle spoke of her mother. Estelle had experienced her mother as never having loved her, as having been rejecting and solely preoccupied with her career, a passionate interest in mathematical research. Estelle's mother had as bedside reading her own doctoral thesis. Working on it was her source of comfort while she was tending to her daughter, and even at the present time she turned to it for solace from an unsatisfactory marriage, immersing herself in her work to forget the increasingly bleak image she saw in the mirror every day.

By an irony of fate, Estelle had been born as a result of an error in calculation. "That mother never loved me," she said. "She found me ugly at birth and often told me she wished I were dead. She made a mistake in calculating the dates, this woman who never makes a mistake." To add insult to injury, Estelle had been born prematurely.

If she did not, now, want to see her son, it was for fear of finding him ugly, of finding herself overcome by the same death wishes as those of her mother. She had so much wanted to put things right, to experience a happy mother–child relationship, but now she was crushed by the thought of a fatal repetition. It was as though the nightmare were beginning all over again. The hoped-for narcissistic replenishment had not occurred. In giving birth prematurely, Estelle had in fantasy become part of the world of calculating, cold, monstrous mothers faced with failure. She was afraid of her child. In order to avoid being such a mother, all she could do was assume the painful role of the monstrous child.

The premature infant attached to life by a thread and to machinery by several threads is, for the mother, a disappointing, hurtful, abnormal child, the cause of a narcissistic collapse. I have learned from these mothers that there is no greater narcissistic suffering for a woman than giving birth to an abnormal child. From the babies, I have learned of the unusual power they hold over their mothers; it is a question here not of secondary but of primary narcissism, a matter of life and death. A baby who does not meet its mother's expectations because it is ill or too small can "inspire" a bad mother.

For Estelle, the repetition of prematurity was unbearable. A child who nurses well causes more milk to be produced and gratifies its mother, who feels that she is "good." A baby who seeks its mother's gaze will attach her to itself much more easily than one who does not look at her, who seems uninterested in her. The child is thus in a way its mother's hypnotist. The encounter is extremely painful when the baby is premature or sick, and guilt, sometimes of terrifying scope, is always in the foreground.

A poor prognosis given by a doctor concerned to tell the "truth" can sometimes have disastrous consequences. For in such cases it is not just the child who is broken, but the mother as well, prevented from mothering that child. For whom is this "truth"? What kind of truth is it, when it is uttered in this way? It is important to try to maintain the fragile bond between parents and children. Even if its life ends there, the child must remain, for itself and for the survivors of the drama, the subject of its own story.

For Sylvain, as for many premature infants, it was the father who, in the beginning, was closer to him. The role of the father is an essential one in all such births, for he is often in the front line, the conduit of the relationship with the baby for the wounded mother. In Estelle's case, however, her father had been absent. But in reliving the despair and the loneliness in which her own mother was immersed, Estelle was finally able to let herself be a mother for her child. The error in calculation that had resulted in her birth was, after all, an act of omission that revealed her mother's desire for a child, a desire that had been fulfilled without her conscious knowledge through the choice of her mathematical symptom.

Sylvain had come, in effect, to comfort his mother and give her strength, to draw her toward himself and toward cure. The more Estelle and I spoke of her history, of her difficulty in moving toward her son, the more Sylvain moved towards her and showed himself to be present and desiring. Children are always in a position to be their parents' therapists, which, as we well know, is not necessarily a good thing for them.

Estelle undertook psychoanalytic work. The possibility of such work in a hospital involves ethical issues, but it is also a matter of the individuals involved. It can yield special moments whose lasting effectiveness can never be known. Everything depends on the analyst, on who he is, on the team, and on the transference that connects them, a bond of truth that is no less true for being unscientific. As Octave Mannoni used to say, truth is like the sun: it shines on everyone, but no one can own it.

References

Aubry, J. (1953). *Les formes graves de carences de soins maternels*. Paper presented to L'Évolution psychiatrique, Paris, January.

Cordié, A. (1991). Le phénomène psychosomatique (P.P.S.) chez l'enfant. *Apertura* 6:55–66.

Cyrulnick, B. (1991/1993). *La Naissance du Sens*. La Villette: Hachette 1991; English translation *The Dawn of Meaning*. New York: McGraw-Hill, 1993.

Dolto, F. (1982). *Séminaire de Psychanalyse d'Enfants*. Paris: Seuil.

——— (1982/1986). *La Difficulté de Vivre*. Paris: Inter-éditions, 1982; Paris: Carrère-Vertiges, 1986.

——— (1985). *La Cause des Enfants*. Paris: R. Laffont.

——— (1990). *Lorsque l'Enfant Paraît*. Paris: Seuil.

Dolto-Tolitch, C. (1990). Accueil et humanisation de l'enfant. In *Enfant de Droit. La Révolution des Petits Pas*, Actes du Colloque de 1990 à l'Unesco, pp. 39–53. Paris: La Harpe, Lierre et Coudrier.

Dor, J. (1989). *Le Père et sa Fonction en Psychanalyse*. Paris: Point Hors Ligne.

Eliacheff, C. (1993). *À Corps et à Cris. Être Psychanalyste avec les Tout-Petits*. Paris: Éditions Odile Jacob.

Faladé, S. (1987). Repères structurels des névroses, psychoses et perversions. *Esquisses Psychanalytiques* 7:29–51.

Fantz, R. (1963). Pattern vision in newborn infants. *Science* 140:296–297.

Ferenczi, S. (1955). The dream of the clever baby. In *Further Contributions to the Theory and Technique of Psycho-Analysis,* trans. J. I. Guthrie, pp. 349–350. New York: Boni and Liveright.

Freud, A., and Bergmann, T. (1945). *Children in the Hospital.* New York: International Universities Press.

Freud, S. (1900). The interpretation of dreams. *Standard Edition* 4/5:1–626.

——— (1909). Analysis of a phobia in a five-year-old boy. *Standard Edition* 10:3–147.

——— (1920). The psychogenesis of a case of homosexuality in a woman. *Standard Edition* 18:146–172.

Freud S., and Breuer, J. (1895). Studies on Hysteria. *Standard Edition* 2.

Gurewich, J. F. (1996). Who's afraid of Jacques Lacan? In *The Subject and the Self: Lacan and American Psychoanalysis,* ed. J. F. Gurewich and M. Tort, in collaboration with S. Fairfield, pp. 1–30. Northvale, NJ: Jason Aronson.

Guyomard, D. (1992). Séminaire de technique psychanalytique. Seminar held at the Centre de Formation et de Recherches Psychanalytiques, Paris.

Jakobson, R. (1971). *Selected Writings.* The Hague: Mouton.

Klein, M. (1961). *Narrative of a Child Analysis.* London: Hogarth.

Lacan, J. (1949). The mirror stage as formative of the function of the I. In *Écrits. A Selection,* trans. A. Sheridan, pp. 1–7. New York: Norton, 1977.

——— (1953–1954). *The Seminar of Jacques Lacan. Book I. Freud's Papers on Technique,* ed. J.-A. Miller, trans. J. Forrester. New York: Norton, 1988.

——— (1958). The direction of the treatment and the principles of its power. In *Écrits. A Selection,* trans. A. Sheridan, pp. 226–280. New York: Norton, 1977.

——— (1960–1961). *Le Séminaire. Livre VIII. Le Transfert.* Paris: Seuil, 1991.

——— (1966). La place de la psychanalyse dans la médecine. In *Le Bloc-Notes du Psychanalyste* 7:9–38, 1987.

——— (1968–1969). *Le Séminaire. Livre XVI. D'un Autre à l'autre.* Unpublished seminar.

—— (1969). Deux notes sur l'enfant. Letter to Jenny Aubry, in *Ornicar* 37:13–14, 1986.

—— (1975). Conférence de Genève sur le symptôme. In *Le Bloc-Notes du Psychanalyste*, 1985.

—— (1977). *Écrits. A Selection*, trans. A. Sheridan. New York: Norton.

Lefort, Rosine (1988). *Naissance de l'Autre*. Paris: Seuil. English translation *Birth of the Other*, trans. M. Du Ry, L. Watson, and L. Rodriguez. Urbana: University of Illinois Press, 1994.

—— (in collaboration with Robert Lefort) (1980). *Les Structures de la Psychose. L'Enfant au Loup et le Président*. Paris: Seuil.

MacFarlane, J. (1975). Olfaction in the development of social preferences in the human neonate. In *Parent-Infant Interaction*, ed. M. Hofer, pp.127–149. Amsterdam: Elsevier.

Mahler, M. (1968). *On Human Symbiosis and the Vicissitudes of Individuation*. New York: International Universities Press.

Mannoni, M. (1964). *L'Enfant Arriéré et sa Mère*. Paris, Seuil. English translation *The Backward Child and His Mother*, trans. A. S. Smith. New York: Pantheon, 1972.

—— (1965). *Le Premier Rendez-vous avec le Psychanalyste*. Paris: Denoël/Gonthier. Republished Paris: Gallimard, 1988.

—— (1967). *L'Enfant, sa "Maladie" et les Autres*. Paris: Seuil. English translation *The Child, his "Illness," and the Others*. New York: Pantheon, 1970.

Mathelin, C. (1993). Les approches psychothérapiques de l'autisme et des psychoses de l'enfant. In *Hommage à Frances Tustin*. Saint-André de Cruzières: Audit.

Misrahi, C. (1991). *La Comtesse de Ségur ou la Mère Médecin*. Paris: Denoël.

Misrahi, C., and Hajlblum, S. (1977). Champ phobique: le petit Hans. *Tel Quel* 70:61–75.

Raimbault, G. (1976). *Corps de souffrance, corps de savoir*. Paris: Edition L'âge d'homme.

Sherrod, L. R. (1981). Issues in cognitive-perceptual development: the special case of social stimuli. In *Infant Social Cognition*, ed. M. E. Lamb and L. R. Sherrod, pp. 11–36. Hillsdale, NJ: Lawrence Erlbaum.

Stern, D. (1985). *The Interpersonal World of the Infant.* New York: Basic Books.

Tustin, F. (1972). *Autism and Childhood Psychosis.* New York: Science House.

———— (1991). Revised understandings of psychogenic autism. *International Journal of Psycho-Analysis* 72:585–591.

Vanier, A. (1992). On observe un enfant. *Journal des Psychologues* 96.

———— (1993a). Avant-propos à "L'enfant et la psychanalyse." *Esquisses Psychanalytiques.*

———— (1993b). Autisme et théorie. In *Hommage à Frances Tustin.* Saint-André de Cruzières: Audit.

Winnicott, D.W. (1941). The observation of infants in a set situation. In *Through Paediatrics to Psycho-Analysis*, pp. 52–69. New York: Basic Books, 1975.

———— (1971a). *Therapeutic Consultations in Child Psychiatry.* New York: Basic Books.

———— (1971b). *Playing and Reality.* London: Tavistock.

———— (1975). *Through Paediatrics to Psycho-Analysis*, pp. 52–69. New York: Basic Books.

Wynn, K. (1992). Les surprenants calculs des bébés. *Le Figaro*, August 31, pp. 17–19.

Index

Contributors

Catherine Mathelin, a psychoanalyst and psychologist, works on the child psychiatry and neonatology units of the Saint-Denis hospitals. She was a member of Lacan's Ecole Freudienne from 1974 until its dissolution, and of the Centre de formation et de recherches psychanalytiques (Center for Psychoanalytic Training and Research) until the founding by Maud Mannoni of Espace Analytique, of which she is currently a member. She is the President of Enfance en Jeu, an association for research and study in pediatrics, psychoanalysis, and pedagogy. In 1995 she established the Consultation des Buttes-Chaumont in Paris, a psychoanalytic treatment and training center.

Judith Feher-Gurewich is a psychoanalyst practicing in Cambridge, Massachusetts, and an adjunct Associate Professor at the postdoctoral program for psychotherapy and psychoanalysis at New York University. She led the Lacan workshop at the Humanities Center at Harvard University for over ten years. Coeditor with

Michel Tort of *Lacan and the New Wave in American Psychoanalysis* (Other Press, 1999), she is the author of numerous articles on psychoanalysis, the social sciences, and feminist theory. She is the Publisher of Other Press.

Susan Fairfield is a translator, editor, and practicing psychoanalyst.

Also of interest from Other Press . . .

OTHER

www.otherpress.com   toll free 877-THE OTHER (843-6843)